The Pleasure of Miss Pym

The Pleasure of Miss Pym

by Charles Burkhart

UNIVERSITY OF TEXAS PRESS, AUSTIN

First edition, 1987

Requests for permission to reproduce material
from this work should be sent to:
  Permissions
  University of Texas Press
  Box 7819
  Austin, Texas 78713-7819

Library of Congress Cataloging-in-Publication Data
Burkhart, Charles.
  The pleasure of Miss Pym.
  Includes index.
  1. Pym, Barbara—Criticism and interpretation.
I. Title.
PR6066.Y58Z597   1987   823'.914   87-5829
ISBN 0-292-76496-0
ISBN 0-292-76501-0 (pbk.)

An earlier version of Chapter 3 first appeared as
"Barbara Pym and the Africans," in *Twentieth Century
Literature,* vol. 29, no. 1, and is reprinted here by
permission.

To ROBERT LIDDELL

Contents

Introduction

Pleasure   Comedy is always with us, but it is a braver form in some ages than in others. It would seem to take courage to laugh in times like ours. But from another standpoint what else is there to write, but comedy? When Faulkner accepted the Nobel Prize for Literature, he said that "Man will prevail," a heroic-sounding but doubtful, perhaps in itself comic, assertion. Faulkner's tragic view is anachronistic: it assumes that people may possibly have dignity or nobility or even interest—all qualities the characters of Beckett would laugh at bleakly.

Comedy is limited in scope, and that is part of its appeal. It is especially limited in the novels of Barbara Pym. In them there are no great white whales or old women bludgeoned to death or decapitated: she is very far from Melville or Dostoevsky or Faulkner. Metaphysics is dated or dead in her world; we escape to a little world of England, of clergymen and spinsters, anthropologists and office workers. They are busy with one another, gossiping, drinking tea, conducting jumble sales, and once in a while, not very often, making love. They have their routines, and it is out of the detachment with which she observes their small self-absorbed rituals that the comedy evolves.

If she is a writer of high comedy—the best in this century, as Lord David Cecil has called her—she is more immediate to us than such masters as Molière, and of course less archetypal and profound; she is more human or less glittering than Congreve or Wilde. This is if only by contrast to place her in select company. If there were not a darker side to her, she would not be there; she would be Angela Thirkell. This darker side is more evident as her novels progress, as it is with other writers, other people. *In Youth Is Pleasure* is the title of a novel by one of her favorite writers, Denton Welch—"darling Denton" (*VPE*, p. 196). Her last novel, written in her late sixties, is called *A Few Green Leaves,* which is a melancholy title. But it is still a comedy.

She wrote because of her own pleasure and because she intended to give pleasure. She had what the French call "le désir à plaire"; Lord David has summed it up rather tartly:

> I think one of the reasons she'll stay, by the way, is that she writes in order to please, and I think a lot of writers now write in order to displease, and they succeed very well.[1]

But her comedy, which was never silly or coarse, was not merely pleasant; it was adult and impeccably intelligent. She had her targets, social and personal foibles, against which her arrows were brightly launched, but she was compassionate; certainly she was not Jonathan Swift. It is the purpose of this book to show just where and in what her pleasure lies, and ours.

Acknowledgments   Even an American may hesitate. In a letter to her old friend Robert Smith in 1968, she wrote, "I am still going on with something, trying to make it less cosy without actually putting in the kind of thing that would be beyond my range (keep *that* and quote it in my biography, young man from the University of Texas!)" (February 9, 1968, MS PYM 162/1). And again, writing to Philip Larkin ten years later about

---

1. A review of *The Sweet Dove Died* in a BBC Radio 4 "Kaleidoscope" broadcast.

the possibility of selling her manuscripts through Rota the bookseller, she said that she "wouldn't like any of my MS handwritten material to go to USA to be pored over by earnest Americans . . ." (March 16, 1978, *VPE*, p. 315). It gives pause. Moreover the most disagreeable character she created is Ned, the American in *The Sweet Dove Died*.

However, earnest and not-so-earnest Americans are now poring over her manuscripts in the Bodleian, where they ended up. Also, her books have become more and more popular in America; there has been a fad. Literary criticism is inexorable. And it interested her; she kept voluminous scrapbooks of the reviews of her books which appeared on both sides of the Atlantic.

I am indebted to these scrapbooks, and to many people. I must first acknowledge my indebtedness to myself. Parts of this book appeared in an essay, "Barbara Pym and the Africans," which I wrote for *Twentieth Century Literature,* and in a talk I gave in Los Angeles called "Text and Subtext in the Novels of Barbara Pym." Both of them have been altered for amalgamation here.

I owe so much to conversations with and letters from Hilary Pym Walton, Barbara Pym's sister, and Hazel Holt, her best friend and executor, that there would have been no book without them. Robert Liddell, a friend of Barbara Pym's since their Oxford days, has been, as for earlier books of mine, the best of mentors. Robert S. Smith, another of her longtime friends, has told and taught me a great deal about her. Colin Harris, a curator of Western Manuscripts at the Bodleian, has answered many an earnest enquiry. I am very grateful to Robert Liddell, Robert Smith, and Philip Larkin for permission to quote from Barbara Pym's letters to them; also to Hazel Holt and Hilary Walton for quotations from their collection of Barbara Pym's writings, *A Very Private Eye;* also to Jonathan Cape Ltd. and Macmillan London Ltd. for quotations from Barbara Pym's novels.

Among obliging friends in my pursuit of Pym who have offered various assistance ranging from encouragement to scepticism or even boredom have been my students and other colleagues, and Jean MacVean, Kathleen Heberlein, Lady Mander, Francis King, William A. McBrien, Marina Greenman, Clive Greenman, Dwight Ashbey, Phyllis Wachter, Benton H. Marshall, Robert Gordon, Ronald Pierce, Ruth Griggs, Irwin Griggs, John Heath-Stubbs, Father Gerard Irvine, Lettice Cooper, Barbara Urban, Suzanne Comer, Nancy Rostron, and Nancy Beere.

Abbreviations   Throughout the book I have indicated the source of quotations either, when it is rather lengthy, in a footnote, or in parentheses in the text itself. Because there are many British and American editions of Barbara Pym's novels, I have indicated the source of a quotation by chapter only, not by page.[2] For example, (5) means Chapter 5 in the novel under discussion. If I haven't given the novel's title in the text I add it to the reference by an abbreviation. For example, (*SDD,* 5) means Chapter 5 in *The Sweet Dove Died.*

Abbreviations for the novels:

> *AQ:*   *An Academic Question*
> *CH:*   *Crampton Hodnet*
> *EW:*   *Excellent Women*
> *FGL:*   *A Few Green Leaves*
> *GB:*   *A Glass of Blessings*

---

2. The chapters in *Crampton Hodnet* have titles rather than numbers; I have numbered them 1–23 for reference purposes.

JP: *Jane and Prudence*
LA: *Less than Angels*
NFR: *No Fond Return of Love*
QA: *Quartet in Autumn*
SDD: *The Sweet Dove Died*
STG: *Some Tame Gazelle*
UA: *An Unsuitable Attachment*

Abbreviations for two other sources:

MS PYM: a manuscript from the Pym collection at the
                    Bodleian Library in Oxford

VPE: *A Very Private Eye*

Barbara Pym (*right*) with her sister Hilary
(*left*) and their mother, 1940.

In the office of the International African Institute in the 1950's.
Photograph by Hazel Holt.

At home in Barnes, 1959.

Barbara Pym (*center*); Hazel Holt (*right*).

Left to right: Monica Jones, Hilary Pym Walton, and Barbara Pym, at Barbara and Hilary's home, Barn Cottage, Finstock, 1976. Photograph by Philip Larkin.

Hilary Walton and Hazel Holt, Philadelphia, early 1980's.

Selling books at a jumble sale in Finstock, 1973.

The Pleasure of Miss Pym

Miss Pym and the World

Her life   Life is "comic and sad and indefinite" (*LA*, 7), remarks Catherine Oliphant, who is the heroine of *Less than
Angels*, and one of the most intelligent and sceptical women
Barbara Pym created. Her own life had more shapeliness than
"indefinite" might imply, at least her literary life; it had a rise,
then a fall, and then a rise again, and the figure in the carpet in
it, its pattern, was her passion for writing. She wrote, she
always wrote, from childhood on, including that period of sixteen years, from 1961 to 1977, when her novels were refused by
publishers.

   Her personal life has been given us in *A Very Private Eye*, the
vivid compilation of letters and notebooks and diaries made
after her death by her sister and her executor in 1984. It is full of
surprises. Although at the age of twenty-nine she was already
poking fun at herself as "the bewildered English spinster, now
rather gaunt and toothy, but with a mild, sweet expression"
(*VPE*, p. 122), she had had at Oxford and continued to have
deep romantic attachments. Love was not her sole existence,
neither was literature, but they are inseparable strands in it. She
was in one way the most autobiographical of writers and in another way the least. The parallels between her notebooks and
her books are innumerable, but there was nonetheless a deep
gulf fixed between the privacy of the former and the more pub-

lic postures of the latter. Only once does she herself appear in a book of her own, and then how obliquely:

> It was at this point that somebody came to the unoccupied table, but as she was a woman of about forty, ordinary-looking and unaccompanied, nobody took much notice of her. As it happened, she was a novelist; indeed, some of the occupants of the tables had read and enjoyed her books, but it would never have occurred to them to connect her name, even had they ascertained it from the hotel register, with that of the author they admired. They ate their stewed plums and custard and drank their thimble-sized cups of coffee, quite unconscious that they were being observed. (*NFR*, 18)

A brief outline of her life is given in the first three paragraphs of the obituary which appeared in the journal *Africa*:

> Barbara Mary Crampton Pym died on January 11, 1980. Born at Oswestry, Shropshire, in 1913, she was educated at Huyton College, Liverpool, and at St. Hilda's College, Oxford, where she graduated in English in 1934.
> During the war she worked in censorship, later joining the W.R.N.S., with whom she served in Naples.
> From 1958[1] till her retirement in 1974 she gave devoted service to the International African Institute, as editorial secretary and assistant editor of *Africa* under the Institute's director, Professor Daryll Forde.[2]

To flesh out these facts there are: the happiness of her life of love and the study of literature at Oxford; her long apprenticeship as a writer which culminated in *Some Tame Gazelle,* the first draft of which dates from 1934 and which was finally published in 1950, when she was thirty-seven. This was followed by

---

1. Actually 1946, when she began working there as a research assistant.
2. *Africa* 50, no. 1 (1980). The obituary continues with a lengthy "appreciation" of Barbara Pym's "modest, gentle, and urbane" personality and novels.

five other novels in a decade of successes. In 1961 Cape and other firms refused to bring out her seventh novel, *An Unsuitable Attachment,* finding it not "trendy" or "with it" enough for the "swinging sixties." Then there were the long frustrations of nonpublication, her illnesses after 1970 leading to her retirement in 1974, her "rediscovery" in 1977 deriving from a *Times Literary Supplement* survey published in January of that year concerning the most underrated and most overrated writers of the preceding seventy years: both Lord David Cecil and Philip Larkin named her as the former. The final three years were years of fame, of the successful publication of *Quartet in Autumn* and *The Sweet Dove Died,* of BBC and other interviews, of articles about her and publishers clamoring for her wares. And then the return of illness, and her death.

What sustained her through failure and was not blurred by success was her religion and its observances: late in life she wrote to her friend Robert Smith:

> On Wednesday Lent begins and there is a day of continuous prayer in the church—one of the blessings of retirement is being able to go to such things in the middle of the afternoon. (March 1, 1976, MS PYM 162/2)

Other friends, with their advice and admiration, always helped: Robert Liddell, for example, beginning in the thirties and forties with the long gestation of *Some Tame Gazelle* (MS PYM 153), and Philip Larkin with his encouragement during the sixties and seventies. Her gallantry, of wit and persistence, was remarkable to the end. On February 14, 1979, on the same day she had had injections for cancer, she wrote:

> In the afternoon I finished my novel [*A Few Green Leaves*] in its first, very imperfect draft. May I be spared to retype and revise it, loading every rift with ore! (MS PYM 80, p. 26)

and later:

> A warm fine Easter, sunshine and things burgeoning. I live still! (MS PYM 81, p. 8)

While at the Churchill Hospital in Oxford or at the hospice where she died, she continued to conceive projects: "A spoilt man of 60—? subject for a short story . . ." (MS PYM 82, p. 2). Moreover there are moments, rare ones, for once beyond irony: "I found myself reflecting on the mystery of life and death and the way we all pass through this world in a kind of procession. The whole business is inexplicable and mysterious . . ." (MS PYM 82, p. 3). She died on January 11, 1980.

How she wrote ". . . I honestly don't believe I can be happy unless I am writing. It seems to be the only thing I really want to do" (letter to Elsie Harvey, October 31, 1938, *VPE*, p. 86).

The way she wrote was the notebook way. She jotted down situations, amusing phrases, bits of dialogue in her little note-books, along with shopping lists (carrots, Ovaltine, cigs), expenditures, social engagements. She did not depend on inspi-ration, though how large a role it played is shown in the differ-ence one finds between the bare notation in a diary and the subtle and polished phrase it ended up as in one of her novels. She gave herself literary advice: "Don't actually *write* anything for a year, but go on making 'copious' notes about everything" (MS PYM 65, p. 18) and personal admonition as when, after an unhappy love affair, she determined to "try to write one de-tached observation each day," which is followed on the next page by her mocking query, "What was the detached amusing observation for yesterday?" (MS PYM 64, pp. 1–2).

After the notebooks, the drafts:

I work straight onto the typewriter, and then I've got a rough typescript I can correct. I usually make just two drafts. Once I've finished a book though, I rather lose interest in it. (Interview, *Eastern Times,* May 25, 1978)

I think that revision was very important to her writing. It is one reason the posthumous *An Academic Question* is the least satisfactory of her novels; it was not revised enough. If there were a scale of revisers, with Dickens, who seldom needed to blot, at one end, and Proust, whose work is one endless revision, one big blot, at the other, she would be in the middle. Comedy of her kind, if not of Dickens', must be honed. In an early letter she said of her novels, "When you start to write one you always wonder if you will be able to make it long enough, but by the time you get to the end it is always too long—I love cutting out bits and crossing out whole pages" (February 21, 1939, *VPE,* p. 88). Two letters to Philip Larkin in the sixties are interesting in this respect:

I have revised *An Unsuitable Attachment*—not very well, I believe and it will need some further polishing before it can be sent to any other publisher. I am also going on with another. I like the stage of having work to do on a book, before one actually has to take positive action, like writing to anyone. Revising and polishing could go on forever. (February 16, 1965, *VPE,* p. 234)

And she asks him:

In what way are you revising it [Larkin's novel *A Girl in Winter*]?—I suppose only in details, because isn't a novel like a poem or a piece blown by a glassblower—once it is formed there is really nothing much you can do about it except tinker with details. (May 12, 1963, *VPE,* p. 217)

Here, where she does not deny the inspiration or inevitability of form, the necessity of "tinkering" remains. And it is more than "details": a look at her unpublished manuscripts in the Bodleian proves how flabby and uncertain her first drafts could be. She has been called a "cameo" writer, and cameos result from expert carving. It is a nice question of balance between the flow of creativity and the fine neat finishing labor.

Cornerstones   It is said to be difficult to make a good person in literature interesting. In life it may be less so, and it is easy with Barbara Pym, and with her it is an interesting if delicate endeavor to trace the correspondences between the pillars of her own personality and those of the people in her fictions. How well she knew herself is shown by the irony she directed both against herself and against the qualities which dominate herself and her characters, most of whom are neither entirely good nor quite bad but of a believable moral variety. If her irony left nothing alone, not even herself, it was never at the expense of sane and sensible judgment.

Modesty is not a modern quality, but though she seems always to have been certain of the survival of her books, as when she jokingly addressed a "Gentle Reader in the Bodleian" in her diary ten years before one of them was published (*VPE,* p. 104), she quite lacked the typical ego of the artist. Some ego is inevitable, in that a writer wants to tell a reader that this is the way the world is, it is as *I* see it, but the "I" of Barbara Pym is a quiet one—one which does not insist nor ever cajoles or proclaims.

There is a charming entry in her diary of July 30, 1976, describing a visit of Philip Larkin to her home in Finstock in Oxfordshire:

> We had tea then walked up to the church to see the T. S. Eliot memorial. So two great poets and one minor novelist came for a brief moment (as it were) together. (MS PYM 76, p. 1)

Part of the appeal of her most attractive characters from Belinda in *Some Tame Gazelle* to Emma in *A Few Green Leaves* is their modesty. They are all women; her men can be monsters of vanity. Yet there is something ludicrous in the self-effacement of Mildred Lathbury, a woman so "excellent" that she's a doormat, or Dulcie Mainwaring in *No Fond Return of Love*, who is shoved around by men and women alike. Both Mildred and Dulcie win out, however, though the victory is ambiguous, since each of them ends up with, or seems destined to end up with, an extremely egotistical man—which has its own irony.

A quality which Dulcie Mainwaring better exemplifies than any other heroine in the novels is compassion. Dulcie carries the tolerance of Barbara Pym to the degree of an obsessive sympathy:

> There were so many lonely people in the world. Here Dulcie's thoughts took another turn and she began to think about the things that worried her in life—beggars, distressed gentlefolk, lonely African students having doors shut in their faces, people being wrongfully detained in mental homes . . . (*NFR*, 1)

and again:

> Then, at Oxford Circus, she had seen a new and particularly upsetting beggar selling matches; both legs were in irons and he was sitting on a little stool, hugging himself as if in pain. She had given him sixpence and walked quickly on, telling herself firmly that there was no need for this sort of thing now, with the Welfare State. But she still felt disturbed, even at the idea that he might be sitting by his television set later that evening, no longer hugging himself as if in pain. (*NFR*, 4)

But two hundred pages later the tables are turned:

> Then it came to her—the man was one of her beggars, a particularly ragged one for these days, who shook with a kind

> of ague and offered matches for sale in Oxford Street. She
> had often given him money, though she had not seen him
> lately. Now he walked briskly in the evening sunshine, wear-
> ing a good suit and smoking a cigarette, not shaking at all.
> (*NFR,* 25)

"Not shaking at all": it was perhaps Dulcie who was shaken, or
should have been.

The outreaches of compassion are a total ethnic freedom in
the air of every line she wrote. No innuendoes or hints of prejudice transpire, no neurotic fears or jealousies, against anyone
not white and English. This does not mean that some of the
blacks are not funny or that the idiosyncrasies of the French or
Americans or Irish or Welsh are, as in a drawing room, ignored.
They are all there, but in a liberal and kindly world.

Yet this very tolerance can be comic. Here is Daisy Pettigrew, a liberal lady in *An Unsuitable Attachment,* entering a
restaurant:

> Whenever she entered a café she always felt obliged to choose
> a table where a coloured man or woman was already sitting, so
> that they should not feel slighted in any way. (*UA,* 21)

And Daisy succeeds in outracing a clergyman to a table where
an African is sitting.

The detachment that goes with tolerance is not the product
of indifference, rather a fundamental decency essential to Pym's
comedy and perhaps to herself. Her detachment is not Olym-
pian, because she was too modest and compassionate for that,
but it can reach chilling heights, nowhere more than in the eery
elevations of *Quartet in Autumn.* Here is Marcia, one of the
quartet, when she sees a man collapsing from a coronary
attack:

It was rather disappointing now to see the man on the pavement attempting to get up, but the ambulance men restrained him and bundled him in and Marcia, a smile on her lips, went back to the office. (*QA*, 4)

And an extended example which again concerns the half-mad Marcia, and which deserves quoting at length because, in its startling and savage detail, it is one of Pym's most remarkable passages:

Marcia turned back into the room where her mother had died. It had been left almost untouched since then. Of course the body had been removed and buried, all that was necessary in that way had been done and the proper obsequies performed, but after that Marcia had lacked the energy to rearrange the furniture and Mrs. Williams, the woman who came in to clean at that time, had not encouraged her. "You want to remember things as they were, not go changing them," she had said. She did not care for moving furniture, anyway. The bed had become the place where the cat Snowy slept until his death, when the black part of his fur had taken on a brownish tinge and his body had become light, until one day, in the fullness of time, he had ceased to breathe, a peaceful end. He was twenty years old, one hundred and forty in human terms. "You wouldn't want to be that old," Mrs. Williams had said, as if one had the choice or could do anything about it. After Snowy's death and burial in the garden, Mrs. Williams had left, the work having become too much for her, and Marcia made no pretence of doing anything to the room. On the bed cover there was still an old fur ball, brought up by Snowy in his last days, now dried up like some ancient mummified relic of long ago. (*QA*, 3)

Once in a notebook Barbara Pym had observed, "Being 'interested in people' doesn't necessarily mean that one is a nice or a kind person. There might be too much of the detachment of the novelist or the sociologist in one's attitude" (MS PYM 72, p. 6). But it is this detachment which gives the edge or cool astringency to her comedy.

Simply in terms of quantity there was a great deal to be detached from, as she increasingly accumulated her data. She never stopped seeing, noting, deducing. If Dulcie is obsessed with compassion, Barbara Pym was obsessed with curiosity. Surely, in no novels ever have so many windows been looked out of. The oddest pages in her diaries are the detective journal in which she chronicled the activities of a neighbor and his friends. This went on for over four years. In *Less than Angels,* Mabel Swan and her sister Rhoda Wellcome watch over the fence on one side their trite suburban neighbors, the Lovells, and on the other, the alarming eccentricities of the anthropologist Alaric Lydgate. Everyone in *Less than Angels* seems to be engaged in private, as with Mabel and Rhoda, or professional curiosity, as with the throngs of anthropologists. Dulcie in *No Fond Return of Love* is both a private and a professional researcher:

> For this was really the kind of research Dulcie enjoyed most of all, investigation—some might have said prying—into the lives of other people, the kind of work that involved poring over reference books, and street and telephone directories. (*NFR,* 4)

It is not an unqualified enjoyment: "Curiosity has its pains as well as its pleasures, and the bitterest of its pains must surely be the inability to follow up everything to its conclusion," as Catherine reflects in *Less than Angels* (1).

All the women in all the novels, even the elegant Leonora in *The Sweet Dove Died,* are normally or abnormally inquisitive. The men are less enquiring. Perhaps it is because they go their own selfish way, and do not need to be. This plethora of curiosity in the novels is curious, and one speculates about it—curiously—in their author.

Other writers Every writer is concerned with other writers, if only to be able to dismiss them with a show of authority. Some are generous, but usually more to writers who are dead than to those who are alive. A novelist who is also a professional critic of other living novelists is in a bind, but Barbara Pym wrote no criticism, and was always kind to her colleagues.

I can find only the rare slightly negative comment, as when, concerning, of all people among her contemporaries, the brilliant Muriel Spark, she thought she herself could write "*A Business of Girls* or whatever, much better than Muriel Spark" (MS PYM 58). Of Margaret Drabble, having just read *The Ice Age* and *The Realms of Gold,* she wrote, "She gives one almost *too* much—but I give too little—laziness and unwillingness to do 'research,' which doesn't seem to fit my kind of novels" (*VPE,* p. 329). In her own novels she mentions, or refers to obliquely, herself, Virginia Woolf, Denton Welch, Elizabeth Bowen, Angus Wilson, Iris Murdoch, and others. Aldous Huxley was an early admiration: after tea with Lord David Cecil she wrote in her diary, "He told me that he had been inspired to write after reading Lytton Strachey's *Eminent Victorians* (just as I had been inspired by *Crome Yellow*)" (MS PYM 77, p. 12). But I find little trace of Aldous Huxley in her early published novels, rather in the very early unpublished *Young Men in Fancy Dress.*

She was and still often is compared with Trollope and Mrs. Gaskell and Angela Thirkell; there is no mention of any of these three anywhere in her writing; but there are traces, I believe, of Ronald Firbank, especially in the very early novel, recently published, called *Crampton Hodnet,* and of Stevie Smith, whom she parodied in letters (*VPE,* p. 11).

She also paid the tribute of parody to Ivy Compton-Burnett, the most formidable and unsparing and, of the great comic novelists, the most unread.[3] But much read by her. She agreed with Robert Liddell that *A House and Its Head* was "remarkably fine . . . but oh what inhuman restraint!": yet she achieved in her own books her own human reserve (letter of January 15, 1936, MS PYM 153). In a letter to Henry and Elsie Harvey of July 2, 1942, she complained, ". . . there won't be a new Compton-Burnett for another year I suppose. It is depressing to go round the bookshops and find how little there is that one really wants to buy" (*VPE*, p. 109).

Dame Ivy, a singular craftsperson, is alien to the basic warmth and tolerance of Barbara Pym. Dame Ivy was tolerant of nothing. But I have found many echoes of the Compton-Burnett syntax, the abstract, and, as if one had an English grammar for foreign students in front of one, the insistent and elementary declarative statement:

> "No, I do not think I deserve your hospitality," said Mrs. Killigrew, getting up. "I have not done good this afternoon. I believe I may even have done harm. I must face that. It will be a burden for me to bear the knowledge that I may have done harm," she added, in a surprisingly light tone. (*CH*, 15)

The phrase "in a surprisingly light tone" is a Compton-Burnett mannerism, especially in the early novels of her long career; eventually she settled for "he said" or "she said" or nothing at all. We hear her in *A Glass of Blessings:*

> "But I've given blood so *many* times," said Mary in a weak bright voice. (*GB*, 2)

And often in *Jane and Prudence:*

3. For one parody, called "Friends and Relations," see *VPE*, pp. 78–80.

"Mrs. Arkright?"

"Yes, she goes in and cooks Mr. Driver's meals, and a very good cook she is. I dare say he'll be having a casserole of hearts to-day," said Mrs. Glaze in a full tone. (*JP,* 3)

As early as 1940 Barbara Pym was writing to Robert Liddell:

The influence of Miss Compton-Burnett is very powerful once it takes a hold, isn't it? For a time there seems to be no point in writing any other way, indeed, there seems not to *be* any other way, but I have found that it passes (like so much in this life) and I have now got back to my own way, such as it is. But purified and strengthened, as after a *rich* spiritual experience, or a shattering love affair. (January 12, 1940, *VPE,* p. 100)

But it did not pass altogether; here is a Compton-Burnett moment in *An Unsuitable Attachment:*

"What my wife means is that it will make it easier to discuss this rather worrying business," said Randolph Burdon hastily.

"Of course I meant that," said Bertha sharply. "Mrs. Ainger would think me very discourteous if I had meant anything else." (*UA,* 20)

The writer most mentioned in connection with Barbara Pym is Jane Austen. It is true that their range was circumscribed, that they were mistresses of wit, that they were very English. But one treads gingerly here. Barbara Pym may have echoed her predecessor:

It is a truth now universally acknowledged that owners grow to look like their pets . . . (*SDD,* 8)

or:

The day comes in the life of every single man living alone when he must give a dinner party . . . (*UA,* 11) and she may have consulted her:

> Read some of Jane Austen's last chapters and find out how she
> manages all the loose ends. (February 1, 1952, *VPE*, p. 188)

She seems to have had her in the back of her mind, as when she
wrote to Robert Smith about *Quartet in Autumn:*

> Don't they say that Jane Austen never has two men talking
> alone together in her novels? I'm afraid I have been bolder
> than that. (February 8, 1977, MS PYM 162/2)

She mentions her far more than any other novelist, and named
her own last heroine after one of Austen's—Emma, in *A Few
Green Leaves.*

But the differences are of degree, of course, and of quality.
John Updike wrote:

> Miss Pym has been compared to Jane Austen, yet there is a
> virile country health in the Austen novels, and some vivid
> marital prospects for her blooming heroines. (*New Yorker,*
> February 26, 1979)

I don't know where one could find "a virile country health" in
any English novelist today, and marriage prospects may not be
vivid but are likely in several of the unmarried heroines—
Mildred Lathbury, for example, and Dulcie Mainwaring.

The difference between Miss Austen and Miss Pym is that
Jane Austen spoke out of an assured and moral culture, while
Barbara Pym is afloat in an ebb tide. Austen's novels are of the
present, her present, while Pym's are nostalgic much of the
time, of an order, a world, a way, a past that impinges—comic
and sad and indefinite—upon the grayness of the present. It
may be a harder task to create comedy among the ruins than it
is to laugh at, but receive, standards that are fixed and flourishing. This is not to debate the relative quality of the two writers;

there are constants of intensity and implication in Jane Austen which place her beyond comparison with almost all later English novelists. All this is, is to say that comparisons only fitfully illuminate or satisfy, and that in fact it is not what has been influenced that we want to know about, but what is unique.

Reviews It may have been the general acclaim by readers and reviewers for Barbara Pym's novels during the fifties that made her rejection by publishers in the sixties especially hard for her to bear. Of the many dozens, perhaps hundreds, of reviews that I have read, the majority are excellent. From the beginning she had a fine press. *Some Tame Gazelle* in 1950 was welcomed by Pamela Hansford Johnson, Antonia White, John Betjeman, and many another known name. She was the opposite of the "Brutalist" school; she was to be recommended "to all who are tired of sex, slums and crime." Only the *Times Literary Supplement*, in the typically tart dismissive note of those days, wrote of *Some Tame Gazelle* that "the book flows cheerfully on with little wit and much incident, and many readers will compare it unfavorably with the earlier novels of Mrs. Thirkell" (July 7, 1950). Later the *Times Literary Supplement* called her third novel, *Jane and Prudence*, "very small beer" (October 2, 1953), but this was a sour note in the chorus of praise. Reviewers' adjectives seem repetitive, because there aren't that many adjectives; one reads "brilliant and charming," "astringent," "cool," "gentle but unerring" over and over; the commonest descriptions of all seem to be "dry" and "detached."

The novels have always been welcome in America, especially in later years, when *Quartet in Autumn* appeared in 1978 along with the re-released *Excellent Women*. The posthumous *A Few Green Leaves* was less admired on both sides of the Atlantic— "minor Pym" one critic called it—as were the two early novels edited and published in the mid-eighties, *Crampton Hodnet* and *An Academic Question*. But *A Very Private Eye,* a year or two earlier, was a bestseller in both America and England.

From the beginning a nostalgic note was struck; *Some Tame Gazelle* was an England that never was, but that one wished had been; more recent reviewers and other critics emphasize what they find to be the socially critical or the feminist aspects of her work. She was not a social reformer or a feminist as such, though there is some persuasive if not finally convincing evidence for such claims.

One wonders if a writer *should* get such predominantly good reviews, both for her sake and for the integrity of criticism. It may not be a good sign; it suggests comfort, not iconoclasm, or that, even though it's been a comfortable voyage, the boat has not been rocked. Did Dostoevsky get good reviews? Did Kafka? Did they get any reviews? But Pym is not Dostoevsky or Kafka, and in some moods one might return to her world more readily than to theirs. Her questions are not grave, severe, or suicidal, and her answers, when she seems to give any, are affirmative and pleasant.

Miss Pym and the World of Her Novels

Geographies   Barbara Pym's world is almost as limited as Jane Austen's. With the exception of a passage to Italy in *An Unsuitable Attachment,* her novels take place in the places she knew best, London and its adjacent counties.[1] Of the twelve published novels, seven are set in London, with now and then an excursion to the country; three are set in the country, with an occasional day trip to the metropolis; one is set in Oxford, and one in a provincial university. Her first novel, *Some Tame Gazelle,* is confined to the provinces, while her last novel, *A Few Green Leaves,* like her third, *Jane and Prudence,* is nearly so.

If even in London her range seems parochial, centering in certain parishes like Barnes or Kilburn or Pimlico, there are office buildings, the Temple gardens, the opera, an art exhibition, and many restaurants. There are excursions to Virginia Water or to the Keats House in Hampstead, and all the means of metropolitan transport are utilized. If it seems a small world it is because it is an inner world where place is far less important than just what happens among people within it. There are no set descriptions of locale in Barbara Pym, alive as she is as to how a house reflects its owner, a flat its shabby or meticulous

1. There are three excursions to the West Country in a chapter or chapters of *Less than Angels, A Glass of Blessings,* and *No Fond Return of Love.* There is an expedition to Dover in *Crampton Hodnet.*

occupant. One would never call her an urban or a rural novelist. It could have happened anyplace.

Love, money, and class   The three staples of the Victorian novel are said to be love, money, and class. Today we might emphasize sexuality, power, and the welfare state. What remains of class distinction is vestigial yet very alive, if not so palpably in America as in England. Does a "lady" sit down with her char-"woman" for a cup of tea and a cigarette? The elision of class distinction in England is much more arresting than in America, which has, if only overtly, its idea of togetherness. Transitional, confused, complicated by the influx of the darkskinned and exotic, the English class system was one of Barbara Pym's impartial discernments.

With her it is a genial, not an exacerbated, concern. The key word in class notation is "suitable." John Challow in *An Unsuitable Attachment* is unsuitable because he comes from a lower class than what his attachment to Ianthe Broome with her privileged background would warrant him normally to aspire to. Ianthe's uncle, the Reverend Randolph Burdon, has a wealthy congregation; speaking of St. Basil's parish, where Ianthe lives (and of which she says, "The congregation tends to be a poor one and there are quite a number of coloured people living in the district"), he remarks (and note that he blames his wife, as men tend to do):

> "Ah well, it was not meant that I should work in such a parish . . . Bertha's health wouldn't have stood any district but W1 or SW1. Anything near the Harrow Road, or the canal, or Kensal Green cemetery had to be avoided at all costs. My particular cross is to be a 'fashionable preacher,' as they say. Bertha is quite right when she says that somebody must minister to the rich." (*UA*, 8)

The particular deflationary technique here, as so often, is the cliché: "Ah well, it was not meant" and "avoided at all costs" and "my particular cross." However, it is Bertha, not Randolph—who is preoccupied at the moment with quince jelly—who most needs to be mollified about Ianthe's marriage, and finally, in her invalidish way, is (*UA*, 20).

In *A Glass of Blessings*, Wilmet Forsyth, the central character, is thinking of a husband for her friend, the foolish but admirable Mary Beamish. She dismisses Mr. Coleman, "the good looking fair-haired master of ceremonies" (4) of the servers at her church, St. Luke's, because "Mr. Coleman was too taken up with his Husky and not quite suitable socially" (19). Mary ends up with a vicar, always a respectable fate.

The cleverest example of snobbery is Professor Felix Byron Mainwaring, a suave and rich old anthropologist in *Less than Angels*. He has definite opinions about his fellow workers in the field:

> Many of them, as he put it to himself, were "not quite out of the top drawer," an old-fashioned expression but one that conveyed his meaning perfectly. He was wise enough not to use it indiscriminately in these enlightened days, however, and his manner to the up-and-coming young men who still gathered round him was gracious and often kindly. After all, it was not his fault that his father had been able to educate him at Eton and Balliol. . . . (*LA*, 1)

Here is the old England mockingly saluted. Most of the people in these novels are of course free of this sort of cant "in these enlightened days" but occasionally, believably and amusingly, it surfaces.

Money, however, is a subject mysteriously slighted. Why is this? We are all accountants; we think about money a good deal of the time: even if their income is not specified, protagonists from Moll Flanders to Leopold Bloom keep track of, calculate, and balance or fail to balance their budgets. If they don't, we suspect their reality. No realistic novelist is too well-bred to talk about money, or at least to imply its egregious eminence. In Barbara Pym's novels we know or deduce that a character here and there has a good income, but of only one, and he is a minor personage, do we know what it is. Consulting Crockford for information on Neville Forbes, a brother of the man she is interested in, Dulcie, the heroine of *No Fond Return of Love,* reads that Neville is "vicar of a parish in North-West London, 'Gross Inc. 626£ and Ho'" (which Dulcie thinks is a "rather jolly-sounding phrase") (6). One almost wants to put it down to a ladylike propriety, this omission of money. One remains dissatisfied, whatever the explanation. It is one of Pym's limitations; it causes questions, such as: How can Aylwin Forbes, Neville's brother, live so well? It is unlikely that he has private means because his background is far from grand, and his occupation is only that of editing a highbrow literary journal, and Barbara Pym knew that intellectual journals do not pay well.

But she knew about love, especially its frustrations and sadnesses, and never scants it as a subject. Sophia Ainger, one of the heroines of *An Unsuitable Attachment,* loves her cat Faustina more than her husband, the clergyman Mark, yet, perhaps in a way because of this, she is deeply concerned with the future of her sister Penelope, a gauche, outrée, and entirely appealing young woman of twenty-five:

> ". . . Oh, Mark, she does need to love and be loved."
> "It isn't given to everyone to have that good fortune," he said rather stiffly, for he often found it difficult to know what to say about Penelope.
> "Oh don't talk like that—it's inhuman. What is there for women but love?"
> "Now, darling, you know there are many things," said Mark, the usual stern note coming back into his voice.

"I've been taught to believe that there are—perhaps I've even seen it, but I don't *know*," Sophia protested. "And mustn't all these things be a second best? Oh, not to God—I know what you're going to say." (*UA*, 14)

Although love may not quite have been, to quote one of the poets Barbara Pym was fond of quoting, "absolute sole lord of life and death," it is the force from which sprang her own compulsions and which compelled the characters she drew from herself.

On a more daily basis, they are compelled by food. In America we eat three times a day, and in England we eat four; food is thus a conscious ritual; sleep by definition is not. She seldom deals with dreams, but her characters are forever preparing a ham mousse or boiling their marmalade too long or timing the roasting of a joint. They are almost as busy with "cauliflower cheese" and "boiled chicken with white sauce" as they are with tea.

The novels are awash with, they are inundated with tea. "'There's a cup of tea in the vicarage,' said Sophia. 'Is there ever *not?*'" (*UA*, 23). When in the same novel, Sophia and companions go on holiday to Rome, they no sooner arrive than Sophia's friend Ianthe says to Penelope, "How I long for a cup of tea!" and the entire English party heads for Babbington's: "Oh, the benison of it . . ." (*UA*, 14).

". . . life has to go on, and I suppose a cup of tea does make it seem to be doing that more than anything," says Father Ransome, an especially sophisticated cleric in *A Glass of Blessings* (18). The drinking of tea can be stoic, a routine placebo, a benison. But all tea is not the same. In *An Unsuitable Attachment* when John Challow begins to woo Ianthe, he looks at her intently and says, "I should imagine *you* would like China tea?" (4). As a matter of fact he is right. A down-to-earth type like the shop assistant Miss Caton in *The Sweet Dove Died* drinks, to her employer's disgust, a "tan-coloured liquid in [a] thick white cup" (9). He himself would have drunk Earl Grey, the most popular tea in the novels. China tea is a preference apparently strictly dependent upon social class, and beyond China tea there is no tea at all; the snob Leonora, also in *The Sweet Dove Died*, goes so far as to abandon it altogether: "tea, a drink she did not much like because of the comfort it was said to bring to those whom she normally despised" (19). But elsewhere tea is like a bell that is eternally, regularly tolled; it is the center of office routine or church routine, and often seems to be more important than either, an end in itself rather than a refreshing recess.

The changing world   Tea holds the changing world together when office routine is a matter of gray people engaged in gray duties and church routine is a few green leaves. The comfort of Barbara Pym's novels has been found to be the stability or timelessness or poise of her world, and her integrity or steadiness of outlook justifies this opinion. But she looked at things sharply, and was alert to record every change from miniskirts to Afros. She knew both the England of Perliknit and Wincarnis and Winceyette and a later England where the doctor had usurped the function of the priest, where television was more important than either of them. She asked herself in her diary, "What is wrong with being obsessed with trivia?" (MS PYM 68, p. 9) and recorded, among much else, the trivia of postwar food shortages ("curried whale," "stag's liver"). People eat very well in her first novel, *Some Tame Gazelle* (which was conceived in the thirties), a fantasy, never-never novel, but when she hit her stride, she charted the changes from Kardomahs to coffee bars, from baked beans and steamed puddings to vegetarian cafeterias and (finally) the delicacies of wine properly "chambré" and a just-ripe-enough Brie.

Altogether she was an acute social historian. In *Less than An-gels* Mrs. Beddoes of Belgravia laments the height of her debu-tante daughter:

> ". . . poor Lalage is five foot *eleven*—girls seem to be enor-mous these days, don't they."
>
> "And to think that they grew up under the Labour Govern-ment and austerity," said Catherine. (*LA*, 11)

Basically her historical outlook was that worse times still suc-ceed the former. In the same novel as the elongated Lalage there is a bright young anthropologist named Tom Mallow who asks himself, "If we lamented the decay of the great civi-lizations of the past . . . should we not also regret the dreary levelling down of our own?" (*LA*, 14). The dreariness, the ca-lamity of history was nonetheless the material for comedy.

The story-teller's art   A writer in Ivy Compton-Burnett's *Daughters and Sons,* a dry lady named Charity Marcon, says that "Books are very like plants. They are better, the more they are weeded, and they come up out of each other and are all the same." Barbara Pym's novels are more different one from an-other than that, but they have their similarities. They are of around the same length, 250 to 300 pages depending on the edi-tion, and the plots tend toward the episodic. "Well, I've never been one for a rivetting plot," she said. "I do plan, yes: situa-tion, people, little things that happen to them" (interview, *Eastern Times,* May 25, 1978). In reviews from the beginning, plot is often mentioned as unimportant; a writer in the *Church Times* said that "People, not plots, are her concern" (November 25, 1977). Yet it is always there: "a line to hang the washing on," as Dame Ivy called it. At least the plots of Barbara Pym are be-lievable, unlike the murderous intrigue of Compton-Burnett's

novels. *Some Tame Gazelle* is the most episodic, made up as it is
of set pieces. Its chapters often begin with the leisurely intro-
duction of a new incident, like "One afternoon Harriet set out
for the curate's lodgings, carrying a large basket. Besides a cake
and some apple jelly, she was taking some very special late
plums which she had been guarding jealously for the last few
weeks" (5) or "It was on the next morning that the Archdeacon
preached his famous sermon on the Judgment Day" (10).

Pym became increasingly adroit at the plots behind the
scenes, developments which are artfully hinted at until at the
end, at their culmination, the reader, as if it had been a murder
mystery, is surprised and says, "I knew it all the time." These
underplots are subterranean love stories, whose quickening and
emergence lead to the happy endings. They can begin with indifference, as with Mildred Lathbury and Everard Bone in *Excellent Women;* at first Mildred even dislikes Everard, but it is the
kind of dislike that leads to liking. Another example is Prudence Bates and Geoffrey Manifold in *Jane and Prudence.* The
best example is the buried attraction between the two crusty
elderly members of the *Quartet in Autumn,* Norman and Marcia. Nothing quite comes of it, except for the house she leaves
him, because the affections struggle only fitfully for expression
in this dark account.

Yet even it has an ending that could not be called unhappy.
Letty, one of the three surviving members of the four, realizes
that "life still held infinite possibilities for change" (*QA,* 24).
Without exception the twelve novels conclude on an upbeat
note, a major, if muted, chord. It comes to be as expected as
her easy use of coincidence, whereby among the millions in
London two old friends chance to meet, or a character looking
out the window of a bus sees two people she knows holding
hands. Our credulity is never strained because our own lives

have plenty of coincidences in them.

At a tea party given by Fabian Driver in *Jane and Prudence,* Jessie Morrow spills tea on the lilac cotton dress of her elegant rival for Fabian's tired attentions, Prudence Bates (18). She wins him. There are funny symbolic tableaux like, near the end of *Excellent Women,* Mildred's first encounter with her new neighbors:

> . . . a small grey-haired woman, holding a tea-caddy in her hand, put her head out of the door.
>
> "I'm Charlotte Boniface," she announced. "My friend Mabel Edgar and I are just moving in—as you can see." She gave a little laugh.
>
> Another pair of women, I thought with resignation, feeling a little depressed that my prophecy had come true, but telling myself that after all they were the easiest kind of people to have in the house.
>
> "Edgar!" called Miss Boniface into the other room. "Come and meet Miss Lathbury, who lives in the flat above us."
>
> A tall grey-haired woman holding a hammer in her hand came out and smiled in a mild shy sort of way. (*EW*, 26)

Tea-caddies and hammers: this use of symbolism is sly if not very subtle, but, one is tempted to say, at least it is not poetic. Barbara Pym admired Virginia Woolf but was not influenced by her orchestration of poetic motifs.

Barbara Pym is more "literary" in another way, and this is an odd aspect of her novels, and might be considered a defect. She herself was so enraptured with the "major English poets" that she takes several of her softer titles from them and her characters drop a quotation as readily as they drink a cup of tea. They are prone to make up titles for novels. They quote unquenchably, from the Metaphysicals to the Moderns. This "literariness" is rather endearing, but it is limiting and to a degree unlikely, and it smells of the lamp. Even Marcia in *Quartet in Autumn,* who is obsessively conversant with the National Health Service, milk bottles, and not much else, can dredge up the odd tag or two. Her coworker Letty quotes "One impulse from a vernal wood" (4). Other characters are inordinately given to Anthony à Wood and other prose masters. Hymns resound throughout the novels.

These penchants have their value in that they establish a recognizable world, one we come to feel at home in. Another means of creating Pym's particular fictional community is the reappearance of characters, or, more likely, mention of them, from one book to another. There are dozens and dozens of examples. After we leave Prudence Bates in *Jane and Prudence,* we find out two novels later in *A Glass of Blessings* that she had for a while been engaged to marry Edward Lyall, the M.P. present at Fabian Driver's tea party, and that she has had at least a flirtation with Rodney Forsyth, who is the heroine's husband in that novel. The characters remain alive but behind the scenes; Pym seldom reintroduces major characters but keeps us posted on what has happened to them in later years. Her last and valedictory novel, *A Few Green Leaves,* is rampant with returns, as if she were tidying up her desk before closing it.

Does a reader welcome these echoes? Philip Larkin did not, but she defended herself:

> I'm considering what you said about bringing characters from one's earlier books into later ones and I agree that one does have to be careful. It can be a tiresome affectation. With me it's sometimes laziness—if I need a casual clergyman or anthropologist I just take one from an earlier book. Perhaps really one should take such a very minor character that only the author recognizes it, like a kind of superstition or charm. (Letter of September 23, 1961, *VPE,* p. 203)

Whatever a reader's reaction, her habit is effective in inviting us from the real world into the world of her novels; it encourages us to become, to use Ortega y Gasset's phrase, "temporary provincials."

A feature of her technique that may have been unconscious but is essential to her irony is her manipulation of point of view, by which I mean through whose eyes we view the goings-on. In *Some Tame Gazelle* we see what is happening mostly through the kind and thoughtful vision of Belinda, but also through her sister Harriet, and nearly everyone else—the Archdeacon, the librarian Mr. Mold, Father Plowman, Count Bianco, the wife of the Archdeacon, Agatha, and even the gardener. We see other people see Belinda, and the gain in characterization is a rich one.

There is everything to be said for multiple points of view, as the practice of most English novelists confirms, but in two of her novels she confined herself to a first-person "I" narrative with the increased intimacy and authority this method of narration offers.[2] We tend to believe what people say directly to us. In the book that followed *Some Tame Gazelle*, *Excellent Women*, Mildred Lathbury tells all, and in the fifth, *A Glass of Blessings*, Wilmet Forsyth is our narrator. Both are very intelligent central voices; Barbara Pym did not attempt such refinements as Henry James, who presented a dark tale through the eyes of an uncomprehending yet intuitive child in *What Maisie Knew*, and whose narrative is manipulated like chamber music in *The Wings of the Dove*. But we can see both Mildred and Wilmet even while they are talking to us and we are listening. Mildred is more like Barbara herself; Wilmet is much less so; neither in

2. In addition, *An Academic Question*, for which both first-person and third-person drafts were written, has been published in a first-person version.

any case is actually Barbara. The result is that the dramatic ironies of *A Glass of Blessings* are more astute than those of *Excellent
Women;* some of the time we hear Mildred's voice as Barbara's,
but we are more sceptical of Wilmet's abilities of observation.
Point of view is not something a reader particularly remarks, it
is more of a matter for critics. Whoever's eyes are, like a camera,
recording, we can hear, sometimes at greater distance, sometimes at less, the author's unmistakable own tone.

The unpublished novels   Barbara Pym published eight
novels during her lifetime, which are, in the order of writing:

   Some Tame Gazelle (Cape, 1950)
   Excellent Women (Cape, 1952)
   Jane and Prudence (Cape, 1953)
   Less than Angels (Cape, 1955)
   A Glass of Blessings (Cape, 1958)
   No Fond Return of Love (Cape, 1961)
   The Sweet Dove Died (Macmillan, 1978)
   Quartet in Autumn (Macmillan, 1977)

She had completed, before her death:

   A Few Green Leaves (Macmillan, 1980)

The novel she had finished in February 1963 was also published
posthumously:

   An Unsuitable Attachment (Macmillan, 1980)

Recently published is a novel written almost as early as *Some
Tame Gazelle:*

   Crampton Hodnet (Macmillan, 1985)

A work of the early 1970's has also appeared:

   An Academic Question (Macmillan, 1986)

There have been various hardback and paperback editions in
England and in America.

   In her papers at the Bodleian are other unpublished novels in
various stages of incompletion or draft. I count seven, of which

three are unfinished:

MS PYM 1	*Young Men in Fancy Dress*
MS PYM 5	*Civil to Strangers*
MS PYM 6/1–3	*Beatrice Wyatt* or *The Lumber Room*
MS PYM 7	the Finnish novel
MSS PYM 8 & 9	the war novel
MS PYM 11	*Something to Remember*
MS PYM 12/1–4	the spy novel

Of these seven, the first, *Young Men in Fancy Dress,* was begun in August 1929, when she was only sixteen. The other six were written when she was still in her twenties. In the 1940's she would seem to have been busy with her service in the W.R.N.S., with the beginning of her long career at the International African Institute, and with a revision of *Some Tame Gazelle.*

The most interesting of the so far unpublished but complete novels is the untitled novel set mainly in Finland. It is a bizarre work in that, though she had never visited that country, it is full of local color (some of it cheerfully inaccurate); she had read about Finland and corresponded with friends who were living there. Technically it has a serious problem with point of view, beginning as it does with the thoughts of a young man named Gervase, who may be the only extended case of masculine outlook in any of the published or unpublished works, but switching abruptly and permanently halfway through to a young woman named Flora. When she was in control of her subject, her characters, and her satirical object, her technique as if effortlessly followed. It is strange after reading a novel of such formal ease and clarity as *Quartet in Autumn* to see her floundering in these unpublished and effortful endeavors. If they are to be published they will require massive editing, of the sort she herself gave to her books.

Some Tame Gazelle   In 1950 Barbara Pym entered the professional literary scene with her hilarious first novel, *Some Tame Gazelle*. It is the story of two sisters, ladies of a certain age— Belinda, who has since university years loved the Archdeacon Hoccleve, in whose parish she is now one of the excellent women, and her sister Harriet, a more outspoken type, a plump pianist with a predilection for young curates, especially if they are attractively convalescent and in need of homemade cakes and other solicitudes. Belinda and Harriet are derived, at considerable distance, from Barbara herself and her sister Hilary. They are comfortably fixed, and lead a comfortable life, Belinda busy with the vicarage garden party, and the handsome Harriet receiving regular proposals of marriage from a melancholy Italian count whose name sounds like an aperitif, Ricardo Bianco. Two highlights of the novel are another proposal which Harriet receives, this one from the librarian Mr. Nathaniel Mold, and the marriage offer made to Belinda by Theodore Grote, Bishop of Mbawawa in Africa. Both are refused, the even tenor of the sisters' days scarcely more interrupted by these events than by the irascible Archdeacon's sermon on the Judgment Day, which disturbs his congregation as much by its recondite literary allusions as by its subject, or than by the Bishop's illustrated lecture on the Mbawawa and their outlandish and even obscene customs. The present curate, a startlingly foolish young man, whose "combinations," as we are told in the first sentence of the novel, "show," is named Donne (*not* pronounced like the poet) and gets married to a lady don (who has made "a most substantial contribution" with her research on *The Owl and the Nightingale* [*STG,* 18]); but Harriet is quickly consoled by the prospect of his replacement, who is "dark and rather Italian-looking, paler and more hollow-cheeked than the others" (*STG,* 22). The village is lively with other characters, such as Edith Liversidge, whom Harriet calls "a kind of decayed gentlewoman":

> "Oh *no*, Harriet," Belinda protested. Nobody could call Edith
> decayed and sometimes one almost forgot that she was a
> gentlewoman, with her cropped grey hair, her shabby clothes
> which weren't even the legendary "good tweeds" of her kind
> and her blunt, almost rough, way of speaking. "Miss Liver-
> sidge is really splendid," she declared and then wondered why
> one always said that Edith was "splendid." It was probably be-
> cause she hadn't very much money, was tough and wiry, dug
> vigorously in her garden and kept goats. Also, she had trav-
> elled abroad a good deal and had done some relief work after
> the 1914 war among refugees in the Balkans. Work of rather
> an unpleasant nature too, something to do with sanitation.
> (*STG,* 1)

Edith lives with her relative Connie Aspinall, who has known
great days as companion to a lady in Belgrave Square, and now
wears fluttery gray draperies, as if in mourning for them, and
"plays the harp very beautifully."

It is a churchy village, where every character is a "character."
Yet most of them are based on prototypes whom Barbara Pym
knew in her university days (*VPE,* p. 11). She transformed
them, heightened their oddities, touched them with the power
of fantasy. It is a village that never was, any more than Cranford
was; one wishes that it had been.

In *An Unsuitable Attachment,* written ten or so years later,
one of the heroines, Sophia Ainger, hears of the sisters Belinda
and Harriet, now elderly, and learns that Count Bianco has
died and left Harriet a property in Italy: "How romantic," said
Sophia. "It seems to be not quite of this age, a story like that"
(*UA,* 14). *Some Tame Gazelle* is a story not quite of this age, in
which little happens, and that may be the point of its appeal. Its
theme, if it can be said to have one, is what Belinda realizes at

the end: "Dr. Johnson had been so right when he had said that all change is of itself an evil . . ." (*STG*, 22).

Crampton Hodnet   *Crampton Hodnet* was the strongest of the manuscripts left to repose in the Bodleian after Barbara Pym's death; when it was resurrected and brought forth in 1985, thirty-five or so years after it was rewritten, it became the weakest of the eleven published novels. The question of whether or not it should have been published at all becomes the larger issue of whether any writer's remains—which writer, which remains?—deserve to see the light. On the one hand, there is something to be said for thoroughness. Any literary scrap of a great writer would be of interest, even a bad poem that there is some little chance may be by Shakespeare. But *Crampton Hodnet* is not *Hamlet*. On the other hand there is enough that is characteristic in it to rejoice her fans. Still it is not a novel with which one would want to introduce Pym to a new reader; it might be his or her last Pym.

Written in 1939–1940, a few years after *Some Tame Gazelle* was begun, it is set in Oxford, and to its author Oxford was still so fresh a memory that Oxford in-jokes or references and a complacent local color abound; it seems to be written more for her Oxford friends than for us. It does not transcend her experiences. *Some Tame Gazelle* does; it was so much worked and reworked that it takes off into fairy tale. What she could have made of *Crampton Hodnet,* had she pruned and polished as she liked to do, we do not know. We do know that she abandoned it; though she spent some time in revising it later on, she never sought to publish it.

Perhaps she thought it was not worth meddling with very seriously. But it does have its definite rewards. There may not be depths, but there is, for one thing, a lively double plot, one concerning Jessie Morrow, companion to the busy, bossy dowager Miss Doggett; and one concerning Francis Cleveland, a don of "Randolph" College (modeled after Balliol), who almost, but not quite, has a midlife-crisis love affair with his beautiful student Barbara Bird. They are all an innocent bunch. Jessie Morrow will be harder and slyer and Miss Doggett much more Lady Bracknell in their reincarnations (under the same names) in *Jane and Prudence,* Barbara Pym's third published novel.

And it has comedy going for it. Jessie is responsible for the sharpest humor. When Jessie, "a thin used-up-looking woman in her middle thirties," is offered marriage by a curate, the Reverend Stephen Latimer, it's the novel's funniest scene:

> "Oh, Miss Morrow—Janie," he burst out suddenly.
> "My name isn't Janie."
> "Well, it's something beginning with J," he said impatiently. It was annoying to be held up by such a triviality. What did it matter what her name was at this moment?
> "It's Jessie, if you want to know, or Jessica, really," she said, without looking up from her knitting.

Jessie rejects Mr. Latimer and recommends Ovaltine (*CH,* 10).

Jessie is wise; she belongs in a later book. When Latimer asks her hopefully, "Are there no sick people I ought to visit?" she replies, "There are no sick people in North Oxford. They are either dead or alive. It's sometimes difficult to tell the difference, that's all" (*CH,* 4). And it is Jessie who says that "Women are used to bearing burdens and taking blame. I have been blamed for everything for the last five years, even for King Edward VIII's abdication" (*CH,* 5).

Unfortunately, Jessie, after her refusal of Latimer, pretty much disappears, and we become occupied with Francis Cleveland and Barbara Bird, a relationship that cannot come to good. The wit falters in the latter third of the book, where the travails of Margaret Cleveland, Francis' wife and an uninteresting woman, approach the genre of "romantic" fiction.

Yet already is adumbrated Barbara Pym's great theme, the involved versus the uninvolved life; and even if this novel is inferior to the canon and may not even belong there, yet it does have its own scrappy amusements.

Excellent Women   To return to the order of publication, which again becomes the order of composition, we come to *Excellent Women*. It is as if Belinda, the heroine of *Some Tame Gazelle,* goes to London, and thereby gains in reality. The new heroine, Mildred Lathbury, is not unlike Belinda; she is a meek, submissive, inquisitive, orderly woman, with a routine of church attendance and volunteer work for "an organisation which helped impoverished gentlewomen, a cause very near to my own heart" (*EW,* 1); as she ruefully describes herself, she is "a woman who was always making cups of tea" (24). Her emotional life consists of her admiration for her vicar, Father Malory, and her friendship with his sister Winifred, both of whom, like Mildred, are gentle types. It seems a settled life, rather dim.

As in so many novels and plays, the story begins with the entrance of alien characters and ends with their departure. Into the flat beneath Mildred's move new occupants, the anthropologist Helena Napier and her husband who has returned from military service in Italy, where he had served as Flag Lieutenant to an Admiral. They are a colorful pair. When Helena first invites Mildred in, she declares, "I hope you don't mind tea in mugs . . . I told you I was a slut" (*EW,* 1). Rockingham ("Rocky") Napier is a charmer who collects girl friends and Victoriana. Both he and Helena are perfectly selfish people, the opposite of Mildred; nor are they churchgoers. Into the Malorys' life—into the vicarage in fact, where she rents an apartment from them—comes Allegra Gray, a pretty widow hard as nails. Helena's profession leads us into the world of anthropology, where we meet the sturdy Esther Clovis, who is to blossom—if a woman who has "hair like a dog" (20) can blossom—in a later novel, *Less than Angels;* the President of a learned society, "a tall mild-looking old man with a white wispy beard, in which some crumbly fragments of meringue had lodged themselves" (10); and Helena's coworker, Everard Bone, whom she would like to be closer than a coworker, a handsome blunt-spoken man who wants a woman to wait on him, whether to cook his dinner or prepare an index. What happens is that Helena and Rocky separate, and then are united again; Father Malory and Allegra are engaged, and then separated; and Mildred ends as proofreader, indexer, and probably more, to Everard.

Mildred tells us early on, ". . . I am not at all like Jane Eyre, who must have given hope to so many plain women who tell their stories in the first person, nor have I ever thought of myself as being like her" (*EW,* 1). Hers is a subtler Jane Eyre story, in that Mildred, unlike Jane, is self-effacing and passive, a pawn to stronger personalities like the Napiers. They use her dreadfully, whether she is packing their belongings or serving as intermediary between them in their quarrels or, worst of all, acting as confidante, that thankless role. "Love was rather a terrible thing," Mildred muses (11), yet she has her triumph in her growing relationship with Everard Bone, who is a Christian as well as an anthropologist, and thus appropriate to Mildred just as the chastened and pious Rochester became to Jane Eyre.

Excellent Women takes place in a much more actual world than the pretty village of *Some Tame Gazelle.* Its setting is Pimlico; its church is St. Gabriel's in Warwick Square (*VPE,* p. 206); it's urban and modern and authentic. It has a structure,

with its neat parallels between Everard Bone and William Caldicote, a finicky gourmet brother of Mildred's school friend
Dora; Everard and William are the possible man and the impossible non-man. After Mildred has her annual lunch with
William, she returns by chance to the same restaurant with
Everard, where by chance they encounter William. At the end
of the novel when Mildred is going to Everard's flat to share
a casserole with him, she again, coincidentally, encounters
William en route. That Mildred tells her story in the first person lures us into her life and her minutely detailed occupations;
it does seem to be a story "quite of this age." And though Mildred is very intelligent, her limitations, especially when con-
fronted with the tantrums of Helena or the suave treacheries of
Allegra, grant us the pleasure of irony. Mildred is an excellent
woman who despite her life of services to others, or more
likely, one infers, because of it, comes into her own.

Jane and Prudence   Prudence, in the next novel, was, along
with Wilmet in *A Glass of Blessings,* one of Barbara Pym's favorite characters (letter to Philip Larkin, January 12, 1964, *VPE,*
p. 223); my own among the heroines is Jane. She is said to be
based on Barbara and Hilary Pym's mother, and one hopes she
is. Unlike most women in the novels she is indifferent to dress,
food, and housekeeping. She has some interest in her daughter,
Flora, and a little more in her kindly husband, the Reverend
Nicholas Cleveland, who has long since come to shrug his
shoulders and accept her oddities. She is fey, poetic, and sudden.

She stands back from life, making fitful forays into it, drop-
ping the line of verse or the philosophical query into the most
ordinary of gatherings, usually with the effect of creating a mo-
mentary unease. She does not communicate on quite the daily
terms of other people. Accompanying her husband to lunch at
the village restaurant, the Spinning Wheel, where they are of-

fered a choice between curried beef and toad-in-the-hole, she blurts out:

> "Oh, dear . . . I'm afraid I don't like curry and my husband can't take toad, so could we just have the soup and a sweet, perhaps?"
> "How would you like an egg and some bacon?" said Mrs. Crampton, lowering her voice. (*JP*, 5)

She recalls one of Beckett's most human characters, Maddy Rooney ("two hundred pounds of unhealthy fat"), in the radio play *All That Fall*:

> Do you find anything . . . bizarre about my way of speaking? (*Pause.*) I do not mean the voice. (*Pause.*) No, I mean the words. (*Pause. More to herself.*) I use none but the simplest words, I hope, and yet I sometimes find my way of speaking very . . . bizarre.

Jane is no fool, rather she is what Americans call "off the wall" or "spacy." She may not always be at home in ordinary language, but one waits for what she has to say; there is always comedy or insight in it and often both.

Prudence, her friend, is "smarter," with her green eyeshadow and red housecoat, than Jane could ever be, but she is not as smart in another sense as Jane, who, herself on the sidelines, follows Prudence's love affairs with absorbed interest. Of Prudence we are told that "she had got into the way of preferring unsatisfactory love affairs to any others, so that it was becoming almost a bad habit" (*JP*, 1). Doomed to romanticism, she does not succeed in snaring the village's leading bachelor, the idle egotist Fabian Driver, losing him to a slyer, wittier, more aggressive woman, Jessie Morrow. Jessie is a good warrior; she says of her employer, the bossy Miss Doggett, that the latter "is a vigorous old lady who has no need of my services as a com-

panion but rather as a sparring partner" (*JP*, 3). It is Miss Doggett who comments:

> "In many ways, of course, Mr. Driver is a very charming man.
> They say, though, that men only want *one thing*—that's the
> truth of the matter." Miss Doggett again looked puzzled; it
> was as if she had heard that men only wanted one thing, but
> had forgotten for the moment what it was. (*JP*, 7)

It is Jessie who remembers what it is, and forces Fabian to the
altar.

Men are an ineffectual bunch in *Jane and Prudence*—Fabian,
and Nicholas the vicar, who grows tobacco and buys soap animals for the lavatory, and Edward Lyall, the habitually ex-
hausted M.P. If they were kings they might be called Fabian the
Vain, Nicholas the Mild, and Edward the Tired. Only Geoffrey
Manifold, who works in the same London office as Prudence,
seems prepared to offer her the one thing women want—whatever that is. Men and women seem more naturally alienated
from each other in *Jane and Prudence* than in the novels that
preceded it; the battle lines are being drawn, and it is a more
experienced eye that judges the fray. It is a small book, but as
Stephen Harvey wrote in the *Village Voice*, "*Jane and Prudence* is
a nearly perfect specimen of the lapidary fiction which can re-
veal more about the essence of things than can books with big,
thumping ambitions" (December 2–8, 1981, p. 56).

Less than Angels   *Less than Angels* is a bigger book than
Jane and Prudence, with many more characters, each sharply
drawn, and the bustle of a huge city around them; much more
plot and a more skillful manipulation of foreshadowing; and a
return to the richer comedy of *Some Tame Gazelle*. More confident and vivacious in tone than *Excellent Women*, which had
also been set in London, it also shows the ever-increasing ob-

jectivity which was to culminate years later in the austere refinements of *Quartet in Autumn*.

Yet behind the antics of the anthropologists in *Less than Angels*—and there are many anthropologists, from the sardonic old snob Professor Felix Mainwaring to the shy young beginning student Deirdre Swan—and behind the suburban mundanities of Deirdre's family in Barnes, there is a sad tale. It concerns the young anthropologist Tom Mallow, his career, and the three women who love him: Elaine, from his Shropshire home; Catherine, the romantic novelist with whom he is living when the story begins; and Deirdre. A key word for Tom can be taken from the clumsy anthropological jargon satirized in the novel: detribalization. Born the eldest son of an old family who inhabit Mallow Park in Shropshire, where he first courted Elaine, he has deserted the tribe and his role in it for the outer world, studied in London for his doctoral degree, and done his field work in Africa. After leaving Catherine for Deirdre, and paying a final visit to Shropshire and Elaine, he returns to Africa and is killed, accidentally shot in a political riot. Elaine remains in Shropshire to breed her golden retrievers, Catherine continues to write the women's magazine fiction which is such a contrast to her generous and sharp sensibility, and Deirdre begins to forget her sorrow in the attentions of Digby Fox, a development which delicate foreshadowings have prepared for from the beginning. Digby is another in the gallery of students, appealingly outlandish, wryly cynical, ambitious, outspoken, and poor.

This theme of detribalization is not deeply exploited, but it is there, the story of the rejection of a traditional family role for a rootless, new, somehow anonymous existence. One does not quite like Tom enough to pity him; he is selfish, he manipulates other people, his death is not resonant, only a snuffing-out.

Nor does one need to pity Catherine, because of her strength of spirit and because she is increasingly drawn to an older anthropologist, Alaric Lydgate, who has retired from the African field, who writes slashing reviews in which most paragraphs begin with "It is a pity that . . . ," who likes to sit at night wearing an African mask, soothed by it and brooding, and who, with Catherine's help, in a gala Guy Fawkes Night scene burns his African notes, which in part have been eaten by white ants and which he never would have published. He is liberated, as Tom was not. Anthropologists, or almost all of them, take themselves more seriously than Barbara Pym's saving common sense would allow. She never condemns them, but her humor finds a wide field in their solemn endeavors.

A Glass of Blessings   *A Glass of Blessings* is the story of a useless woman. After Belinda or Mildred, Wilmet Forsyth is a model of elegant idleness. She is a beautiful woman of thirty-three who has everything: money, clothes, house, a best friend, an admirer—her best friend's husband—and a civil servant named Rodney for husband; but, perhaps because of all this, she is restless. George Herbert's poem "The Pulley," from which the title of this novel is taken, is recalled in the last chapter:

> When God at first made man,
> Having a glass of blessings standing by . . .

Wilmet tells her story in the first person, a mild, witty, yet obtuse narrative. She seems to be the only person in the novel who does not know that the man she is attracted to, Piers Longridge, who is attracted to her, but in a different way, is homosexual. When she learns at last that the person he shares a flat with is not a woman or coworker but a bouncy boy named Keith, the revelation is only one of the educations she undergoes. She has always known she was useless: she says that "It makes one feel rather useless" not to have children (3), and when Piers points out that no one will miss her if she doesn't return home in time for tea, she again admits it: "'No,' I said comfortably. 'I'm useless'" (5). What she more deeply comes to realize, after having learned of Piers and Keith, and of the forthcoming more orthodox unions of her friend Mary Beamish with Father Ransome and of her mother-in-law Sybil with an elderly archaeologist, Professor Arnold Root, is that, as she says, ". . . life had been going on around me without my knowing it" (20). She has been naïve: "I had always regarded Rodney as the kind of man who would never look at another woman. The fact that he could—and had indeed done so—ought to teach me something about myself, even if I was not yet quite sure what it was" (22). It is not exactly what it was that is important, rather that her outlook has been enlarged.

A Glass of Blessings is composed of contrasts between Wilmet and other women. Her mother-in-law is as agnostic and brusquely outspoken as she is not; her best friend Rowena has children and runs a lively household; another friend, Mary Beamish, is so useful and excellent a woman—looking after a horrendous old mother, giving blood, working as housekeeper at a place of retreat for church people—that once in a while she irritates Wilmet.

Sybil, wise as her name, introduces the topic of male homosexuality early in the novel with her blunt remarks about the scandals involving the clergy reported in the gutter press. The subject is increasingly to occupy the later novels, and it has not been absent from the earlier ones. There is the tragicomic pair of Piers and Keith, and the totally comic figure of Wilf Bason, a gabby gourmet cook (gourmet men in these novels are often homosexual types) who has a head like an egg and steals a Fabergé egg from his employer, Father Thames. But Father

Thames' main interest in Wilf Bason is the latter's finesse with cuisine; once he confided to Wilmet: "'Do you know,' he lowered his tone, 'he has promised us a coq au vin?'" It is Father Thames who says, "I have been a priest for over forty years and I have never been able to take Indian tea" (*GB*, 4).

This novel, like all of the novels, rejoices in many a comic minor character—which may be the main pleasure some people find in reading them. There is Mary's mother, "old Mrs. Beamish, large and black" (*GB*, 4). There is Miss Prideaux, also elderly, who lives on "her vivid memories of life as a governess in Europe in the grand old days," and whom we meet in a typical vignette:

> Miss Prideaux was of the generation which wears a hat in the house for luncheon and tea, and she now came forward to greet us wearing a little black toque to which a bunch of artificial Parma violets had been pinned at a rather rakish angle. Her cheeks were, as usual, very heavily rouged. (*GB*, 2)

And there is Miss Prideaux's ancient swain, Sir Denbigh Grote, a retired diplomat complete with monocle:

> "Was I ever in Lisbon?" Sir Denbigh repeated. "Lisboa—ah, yes, but many years ago. The climate is delightful, but the language is very difficult—perhaps too difficult for ladies." (*GB*, 2)

After a candlelight service in their church, St. Luke's, Miss Prideaux says to Wilmet, "So beautiful all those candles . . . but rather dangerous. I am always so afraid of fire, and Sir Denbigh's candle was burning dangerously low" (*GB*, 18).

From Miss Prideaux and Sir Denbigh to Mary Beamish and Father Ransome, from Piers and Keith to Sybil and Professor Root, *A Glass of Blessings* has some sort of love affair for everyone but Wilmet. Yet in the end she is content, having learned whatever she has learned, having, by her grace and wit, survived:

I turned into the street where our new flat was, and where I knew Rodney would be waiting for me. We were to have dinner with Sybil and Arnold that evening. It seemed a happy and suitable ending to a good day. (*GB*, 23)

No Fond Return of Love   *No Fond Return of Love* is a falling-off from the two novels it followed, *Less than Angels* and *A Glass of Blessings*. It has the usual merits of form and precision, irony and insight, but the male characterization is unpersuasive, and there is a repetition of familiar motifs. Dulcie Mainwaring is like earlier women in her curiosity, here raised, or sunk, to the level of prying, and in her passion for every beggar or mendicant, here almost foolishly sentimental. She is an indexer, editorial assistant, and bibliographer, and her life, suited to her occupation, is as quiet as Mildred Lathbury's. It takes on interest when she attends a learned conference (where there are talks like "Some Problems of an Editor" and "Some Problems of Indexing") and meets there both the editor of a literary journal, Aylwin Forbes, and a scatty and awkward young woman named Viola Dace (she has been christened Violet, but began to call herself Viola at the age of seventeen [*NFR*, 1]), who has a crush on Aylwin. Viola becomes a tenant in Dulcie's large suburban house, as does Dulcie's niece Laurel, who is fresh from the country and is eager not for suburbia but for the splendors of Notting Hill Gate and the coffee bars of Chelsea or Soho. Aylwin, who is separated from his wife, Marjorie, an ordinary pretty woman who wears pink or mauve sweater twin-sets (20), in rapid succession toys with Viola, pursues Laurel (who thinks he is an old man), is provided with grounds for divorce by Marjorie, and finally settles on Dulcie. The original title of the novel was *A Thankless Task*;[3] it would be a fitting title to a

3. Letter to Robert Smith, October 21, 1960, *VPE*, pp. 200–201.

sequel about Dulcie's marriage to Aylwin, if it is to come to that. But she has pursued him through Crockford's, telephone directories, and his mother's hotel in the West Country, and what she gets is what she wants, even if she deserves much better. He lacks her wit, unselfishness, and reliability, but he is better than nothing after the "broken heart" of her broken engagement with an insipid art dealer, sketchily drawn, Maurice Clive. That is, if anything is better than nothing. It is a rueful story, though the three women attain their goals; it is perhaps rueful in another way that they feel they must have them. In any case Dulcie ends with Aylwin, Laurel with a bedsitting room which she will decorate with posters of pop stars, and Viola with an energetic and courtly Viennese emigré named Bill Sedge, who is a knitwear buyer for a chain of dress shops.

Perhaps the funniest character in the novel is a simply dreadful poodle named Felix; or it may be his gushing owner, Dulcie's neighbor Mrs. Beltane: "But Felix has been very naughty and I don't think Miss Mainwaring is going to let him have one of his favorite petit-fours, are you, Miss Mainwaring?" Upon which, when Dulcie suggests a plain biscuit, Mrs. Beltane replies, in a doting tone, "No thank you, we wouldn't, would we, Felix . . . We don't like plain biscuits, do we. *We* like petit-fours" (*NFR*, 5).

And there are other brief appearances of people we are glad to encounter: Mrs. Forbes, Aylwin's sharp-tongued and coarse old mother, or the Senhor MacBride-Pereira, a Brazilian who is fond, particularly fond, of Elvas plums, and of Mrs. Beltane, whose tenant he is, or maybe more than tenant. Yet these amusing types seem irrelevant; they walk on, do their turns, and step back into the wings. *No Fond Return of Love* is a readable, likable novel but suffers when compared with *Less than Angels, The Sweet Dove Died,* or *Quartet in Autumn.*

An Unsuitable Attachment   If she has neither child nor career, no duties but those of affectionate spouse to a quiet clergyman, what is a woman to love? Sophia Ainger adores her cat Faustina, though this is not the unsuitable attachment to which the title of the next novel refers.

Nor was it the first title. There were at least thirty others recorded in the notebooks, mostly to do with lemons: *A Plate of Lemons, Wrapped in Lemon Leaves, The Lemon Leaves, A Lemon Spring, Under the Lemon Leaves, A Prospect of Lemon Leaves, Hidden in Lemon Leaves*, and so on. Lemons dominate a mysterious scene when Sophia is visiting her aunt, who has both lemon orchards and a lover, in southern Italy. It is an epiphany, but what the epiphany is about isn't quite clear. Is it Sophia seeing into the heart of things? Is it her recognition of the secret beauty one might have found, but she has not, in life?

The emphasis placed on this incident, which is of a lyricism unique in the novels, suggests that Sophia may have been intended to be the principal character, not her friend Ianthe Broome, whose attachment to John Challow her friends and family find unsuitable. Ianthe is better bred than John, with her Hepplewhite chairs and Pembroke table, her coats of moleskin and gray squirrel, while John lives in a shabby Pimlico bedsitter and wears shoes that are too pointed; and she is five years older than he. She defends herself:

> ". . . people *do* marry quite late in life."
> "I always think that's such a mistake," said Sophia. "You seem to me to be somehow *destined* not to marry," she went on, perhaps too enthusiastically. "I think you'll grow into one of those splendid spinsters—oh, don't think I mean it nastily or cattily—who are pillars of the Church and whom the Church certainly couldn't do without."
> Ianthe was silent, as well she might be before this daunting description. (*UA*, 17)

Ianthe is not daunted, and marries the man who is too young and too common and whom she loves.

Ianthe is less interesting than Sophia, who is a stranger study altogether. Early in the story, a neighbor of hers, who is sister to a veterinarian, is watching Sophia: "She makes too much of that cat, Daisy thought, for a young woman that is. It was a pity she had no children . . ." (*UA,* 2). When she is in Rome Sophia says about Faustina, "I shan't worry really, but she's all I've got" (12). This, in the presence of her husband. In truth she misses Faustina passionately: ". . . she could almost smell her fresh furry smell and her warm sweet breath" (17). She asks Ianthe in the same conversation quoted above, the most intimate they have, "Do you know, I often ask myself, did I do wrong to deprive Faustina of the opportunity of motherhood? You knew that she'd had the operation?" (17). One remembers that "Faustina" suggests a Roman empress or two of dubious ancient reputation.

Sophia is unfulfilled, and will be, and she is a fascinating psychological case. But the book, as is obvious from its final title, is intended primarily to concern Ianthe and John, and this was a point in Anne Duchêne's review in the *Times Literary Supplement:* ". . . the book lacks a central coherence, in that the two protagonists of its 'unsuitable attachment' are its least vigorous and convincing components" (February 26, 1982, p. 214).

The peripheral characters are indeed excellent, whether Ianthe's gauche and nubile younger sister Penelope or Rupert Stonebird, a professor of anthropology who ventures into life but usually steps back quickly into his study, or the waspish librarian Mervyn Cantrell, another effete gourmet, or the elegant Basil Branche, another effete curate. Possibly, however, the novel was refused by publishers in the early sixties, and not published until the eighties, after its author's death, because it

wasn't revised enough. Its focus, theme, and wit were not clari-
fied and sharpened. It is the closest of any of the novels to the
notebooks themselves, so close that the chapters in Rome
(where Barbara Pym had attended a meeting of the executive
council of the International African Institute in the spring of
1961) sound here and there like a travelogue ("The next few
days passed happily and profitably in a whirl of sightseeing"
[16]). Yet in 1982 it was certainly publishable, if for its comedy
alone, and certainly welcome; and if it has deficiencies, they are
relative ones, flaws from our high expectations, not failures.

The Sweet Dove Died Barbara Pym kept on writing. Although she defended her own manner and choice of content,
rejection profited her in that *The Sweet Dove Died,* which she
completed in the late sixties,[4] is a harder, tougher book. No
matter what painful autobiographical experiences lie closely behind it, it is so objective that, for the first time, little or no in-
gredient of fantasy or wish-fulfillment lies within her heroine.
Its triumph is that the heroine this time is not a likable person,
yet we come to sympathize with her and even to pity her in her
defeat. She has style and she has courage and they carry her
through. Alone among the heroines she has no sense of humor;
the comedy of the novel lies elsewhere.

That Barbara Pym's study to extend her range beyond do-
mestic love comedies was quite conscious is shown in her
letters of this period. A key word seems to have been "cosy."
One wonders who had complained. She wrote to Philip Larkin
of the first draft of *The Sweet Dove Died,* "The friend who has
read it thinks it almost a sinister and unpleasant book, which
may be all to the good. I didn't try to make it so, but tended to
leave out boring cosiness and concentrate on the darker side"

4. *The Sweet Dove Died* was written earlier but published later (1978) than
Quartet in Autumn (1977).

(December 7, 1967, *VPE*, p. 244). Two years later, after "revising and 'improving,'" she wrote him, "I have cut out a lot of the characters, ruthlessly suppressed (or tried to) all 'cosiness' and am now struggling with the last difficult chapters, which are new" (letter of September 19, 1969, *VPE*, p. 251).

She wanted to be, she knew that she was, more than a "lady novelist" who was "good bedside reading"—which had been, as she knew, an easy way to characterize her in the past. Writers of comedy are thus afflicted when seriousness is confused with solemnity. She could not be solemn.

The Sweet Dove Died is the dark comedy of a woman, Leonora Eyre, no longer young, but with the charm of beauty past its prime, to whom a little Victorian flower book or a fruitwood mirror carved with cupids is more desirable than to be the object of sexual desire. In fact she is frigid: "She did not like being kissed by women, or indeed anyone very much" (2). In a way she knows that she is: "But had there ever really been passion, or even emotion? One or two tearful scenes in bed—for she had never enjoyed *that* kind of thing—and now it was such a relief that one didn't have to worry anymore" (2). On a country expedition to Virginia Water with one of her elderly admirers, Humphrey Boyce, an antique dealer, she averts her gaze from a totem pole: "What a hideous phallic symbol, Leonora thought . . ." (5). When Humphrey tries to embrace her, she feels "sudden panic" (11). She sees "a sweet little man" in every male from a park attendant to a black taxi driver to the foreman of a furniture repository, thus reducing all males to non-threatening impotency. She associates sex with squalor; her favorite opera is *Tosca;* she is a romantic perfectionist:

> "Yes, I suppose one feels that life is only tolerable if one takes a romantic view of it," Leonora agreed. "And yet it's wicked, really, when there's all this misery and that sort of thing, but

one feels so helpless—I mean, what can one *do*? As it is one tries to lead a good life . . ." She paused, dissatisfied with the phrase, for somehow it conjured up a picture of Miss Foxe [Leonora's tenant] going out to church early on a Sunday morning and that had not been at all what she meant. "One enjoys the arts and gives something to charity, of course, and"—here she bowed her head over her crème de menthe— "one loves people to the best of one's ability . . ." (*SDD*, 11)

It is a devastating passage.

Barbara Pym wrote in her notebook:

Blurb for my nearly finished novel. What is it about? The struggle of two women, unknown to each other, to get a young man who doesn't really want either of them. (MS PYM 63, p. 14)

The two women are Leonora and the far younger Phoebe; the young man is James, Humphrey's nephew whom he is training in the antiques trade. James is a callow, unformed, well-bred youth whom Leonora takes under her wing. She likes to stroke his hair while, at her feet, he reads poetry aloud to her in his beautiful voice. Phoebe is no threat to Leonora. The threat is Ned, an American who is in England for a while, and who is a particularly obnoxious young man, with his voice like a gnat, his Mitsouko, his falsity and flattery, his promiscuity, his capriciousness, his insinuating questions. He becomes James' lover for a while, then drops him for other prey. Leonora is left to her pain: "I am utterly alone, she thought" (*SDD*, 22). ". . . growing unhappiness had made her more sensitive" (19) to the solitude and pathos of others, but she solaces herself for her losses by a return to exquisiteness. In a review published in the *Washington Star* on May 27, 1979, Larry McNurty makes a very just comparison between Barbara Pym and Henry James:

. . . in *The Sweet Dove Died* she is writing at the top of her powers about a subject that has often engaged her: that subject is the unlived life. At one point the book echoes *The Ambassadors*. Leonora, who should have been a Madame de Vionnet, remains, like Strether, on the sidelines, diminished by her own insistence on perfection. She won't accept the mess that emotion entails and thus is left with the small and not always comforting perfection of her rooms, her objects, and her arrangements. Her plight is poignant, rather than tragic . . .

The sexual career of young James is carefully foreshadowed early in the first chapter when, at a Bond Street sales room, "a tall man with a slightly raffish air" keeps staring at him. Later, Miss Caton, Humphrey's shop assistant, says, "Oh, that man— he's always hanging round here . . . You don't want to have anything to do with people like that" (*SDD,* 9). And in Leonora's history there are the usual parallels and contrasts. Leonora's tenant, Miss Foxe, has found contentment with her faith; but Leonora "never went near a church" (22). Leonora's friend, the frowsy and motherly Meg, is in love with a gay young man named Colin who periodically and predictably deserts her to her blubbering sorrow (she keeps a bottle of Yugoslav Riesling in the fridge against his return: "it's his favourite wine" [4]). Leonora's neighbor Liz, scarred survivor of an ugly marriage, is a symbol of what a disaster that institution can be, and now lavishes her love on the Siamese cats she breeds. Leonora can be none of these, neither a churchwoman nor a mother surrogate nor a cat lover. One can see her becoming more brittle and more perfect as she ages. Until she dies; yet, even then, "there was no reason why one's death should not, in its own way, be as elegant as one's life, and one would do everything possible to make it so" (2). On her deathbed she will still be the implacable stylist. One admires her mania, and one admires the brilliant believability with which Barbara Pym endows her—so alien to herself, so alienated from the ordinary realities of life.

An Academic Question   Like *Crampton Hodnet, An Academic Question* was part of the trove which students have discovered among the manuscripts given to the Bodleian by Hilary Walton after her sister's death. Published in 1986, it made, along with *An Unsuitable Attachment, A Few Green Leaves,* and *Crampton Hodnet,* the fourth novel to be published posthumously. At least one more manuscript, the early novel set in Finland, is still to appear.

An Academic Question exists in two versions, which date from 1970 to 1972. They were combined and edited into the published version by Pym's literary executor, Hazel Holt. The title, a good one, is Holt's.

In fact, all credit must go to Hazel Holt. The only triumph of *An Academic Question* is its editing. Again like *Crampton Hodnet,* one wonders if it deserved resurrection, and some of the reviews doubted that it did. In fact A. S. Byatt, in the *Times Literary Supplement* of August 8, 1986, described it as "a mistaken attempt . . . thin and unappealing." Although other critics have been somewhat kinder, it is easy to see why its author abandoned it, and hard to believe that this pale exercise was followed in the same decade by the publication of two such rich and assured accomplishments as *The Sweet Dove Died* (completed in 1968 or 1969; revised in 1977 [*VPE,* pp. 213, 337]; published in 1978) and *Quartet in Autumn* (published in 1977).

She is both too close to her subject and too far from it. There are caricatures of people she knew, like the forty-ish dandy named Coco, who is interested in clothes, in his mother, and in himself; there is an edge of malice in his characterization, her usual admirable detachment having failed her. She tried to be objective—the first version is written in the first person, the second in the third—but she did not quite succeed. And she did not know enough about academe, whatever her thorough knowledge of learned societies like the African Institute. They are related but not the same. There are apt sketches of scholars at the provincial university where the novel is set, but the academic scene has elsewhere been so thoroughly and comically dissected by everyone from Mary McCarthy to Randall Jarrell that the pretensions of professors and the shenanigans of students here seem only an echo of better books.

The plot has to do with a young woman named Caroline Grimstone, whose husband is a lecturer very much on the make, to the extent that he steals a manuscript to use in an essay of his own. The theft is never discovered, and the manuscript is finally destroyed in a fire which results from the pranks of students on Guy Fawkes night. Alan Grimstone is amoral and thoroughly disagreeable; he addresses scarcely one amiable remark to his wife—usually he nags—throughout their pointless little story. There are precious louts and egomaniac monsters among the men in the other eleven novels, but one can indulge them because they are funny. Alan isn't.

Caro's predicament, outside that of her husband, is that she is rather a nothing character. She is a sort of drifter, without a primary interest in work or family. She likes to gossip with Coco; she is interested enough in Alan to be jealous of other women he favors; she now and then performs little acts of kindness; but she curiously lacks temperament. She is not representative of anything in particular, unless of the unfulfilled, unplaced, or unplaceable young woman of our time, halfheartedly feeling herself hemmed in and powerless: a portrait of female futility unrelieved by passion or by religious or other devotion.

There are indeed Pym touches of sharp witty observation. There are the old interests in anthropology, hedgehogs, and jumble sales; characters from other books, as is their wont, re-appear, like Sister Dew and Digby Fox, or are mentioned, like the mighty Esther Clovis, now alas dead. There are an amusing au pair named Inge and her charge, Caro's four-year-old Kate, who has a Swedish accent. And there is one robustly eccentric elderly woman named Dolly Arborfield. A dinner party guest discovers a hedgehog skin on Dolly's sofa:

> "Yes, I found it in a drain," said Dolly coming into the room and taking it from him. "Goodness knows how long it had been there—see, it's quite dried, all the flesh gone. What hap-pened to that poor creature? That's what we must ask our-selves." (*AQ*, 5)

The fault of *An Academic Question* may simply be that it was not sufficiently revised: it is not thoroughly realized. To com-pare any page of it with a page of *The Sweet Dove Died* or *Quartet in Autumn* is to move from hesitation and lack of focus to a much more complex and competent inventiveness. Its in-terest to a Pym reader may be in what it is not rather than what it is, but this is scarcely a very compelling attraction.

Quartet in Autumn   It is difficult to imagine two novels by the same author more different than *Some Tame Gazelle*, the first one Barbara Pym published, and, published seventeen years later, *Quartet in Autumn*, her last major accomplishment. The follies exuberantly depicted in the first novel have become, in this one, the foibles of a foursome of elderly citizens por-trayed with a cool, distant, and at times sinister wit. Instead of attending a vicarage garden party where coconuts are shied, marrows are arranged in monumental display, and the heart of Belinda is gladdened because she has tea with her impossible

friend, the Archdeacon, we are in the gray world of bureau-
cracy with four civil servants, hopelessly human and ordinary,
whose work is so anonymous that it is never specified. An iron
routine has set in of Underground and buses, of shared tins of
Nescafé, of gossip, bickering, and sarcasm. Yet beyond lies the
peril of retirement: the two women of the quartet, Letty and
Marcia, reach the compulsory age and are cast loose in a world
which now lacks its arid but occupying center, and it is their
subsequent fates, the one undecided but the other chilling,
which we follow. *Excellent Women* and *Jane and Prudence* and *A
Glass of Blessings* also had their authoritative accounts of office
life—Barbara Pym knew all about it—but they are exploited
for their humor, as when Mildred Lathbury's friend William
Caldicote complains, "They've moved me to a new office and I
don't like it at all. Different pigeons come to the windows"
(*EW,* 8).

Routine is both stale and sustaining to Letty and Marcia;
what are they to do with freedom? Letty's life is a gradual di-
vestiture of what has made it up: her job (she must retire); her
room (she must move); her best friend, Marjorie (with whom
she had planned to retire in the country, but who becomes engaged to a clergyman). Death is everywhere in this novel.
When Letty visits Marjorie, "On their walks she was always the
one to find the dead bird and the dried-up hedgehog's body or
to notice the mangled rabbit in the middle of the road when
they were driving" (*QA,* 5). Rather than a retirement home, it
would be "better to lie down in the wood under the beech
leaves and bracken and wait quietly for death" (17). Letty floun-
ders, dabbling in "serious" books, church attendance, and television; but at last falters her way to a sort of dim and incon-
clusive liberation. It is Marcia, mad or nearly so, who starves
herself and dies.

The history of her disintegration is powerful and relentless. Robert Liddell says that Marcia and the Archdeacon are "Barbara Pym's greatest creations of character, the former tragic and the latter comic."[5] There is a clinical acuteness to the portrayal of Marcia which seems more French than English in its naturalistic cool detail. She cuts herself off from humankind—from Letty, who could have been a friend, and from Norman, who could have been more than a friend, and from officious social workers and neighbors and bus conductors. Her mania is for the material, for milk bottles and rows of tinned foods arranged by proper category and unworn articles of apparel and plastic bags. As she becomes more and more emaciated and weird in appearance, her mind a mishmash of prejudice and hostility, her ties to humanity contract to her remote adoration of her surgeon, Mr. Strong. Her death is a bizarre and even triumphant apotheosis of her obsession with the medical; she laments the absence of a bell ringing on the ambulance that takes her to her deathbed. All subconsciously she has killed herself; she is the ultimate case of disinvolvement.

Yet, even though she described it in her notebooks as "austere and plain" (MS PYM 73, p. 22), *Quartet in Autumn* is still a comedy, and recognizably a comedy by Barbara Pym. When Letty returns to her room after Marcia's funeral service, she is offered refreshment by her landlady, Mrs. Pope, and replies, "'I think just a cup of tea . . .' There was something to be said for tea and a comfortable chat about crematoria" (21). All the principals have their Pymian oddities, including the men—Edwin, with his incessant round of attendance at High Church services, and Norman, with his truculent suspicion of everything and everybody. Edwin has almost forgotten that he is a wid-

5. In a conversation in Athens in March 1985.

ower; buying some reading material for a train journey at a station bookstall, he sees "a colourful range of magazines on the
counter, some of which displayed the full naked breasts of
young women, enticingly posed. Edwin looked at them dis-
passionately. He supposed that his wife Phyllis had once had
breasts but he could not remember that they had been at all like
this, so very round and balloon-like" (5). Norman vents his
spleen by kicking automobiles or sneering at social workers.
The futility of the elderly four is contrasted with the vitality of
the blacks they encounter, the saucy Eulalia in their office, and
the Nigerians, Bishop Olatunde and family, who are new
neighbors of Letty and whose religious services, with their
"bursts of hymn-singing and joyful shouts," bother her:

> "I wonder if you could make a little less noise?" she asked.
> "Some of us find it rather disturbing."
>   "Christianity *is* disturbing," said Mr. Olatunde.

When his wife, "a handsome woman in a long brightly-coloured
dress," invites Letty to join them for supper, Letty thanks them
politely, saying she has already eaten:

> "I'm afraid you would not like our Nigerian cooking," said
> Mr. Olatunde, with a touch of complacency. (*QA*, 7)

The novel at one point was named *Fourpoint Turn*, but the
title *Quartet in Autumn* suggests the proportion and musi-
cality of its structure. It is a "late quartet" in its bold technique;
we hear one voice after another, contrasting, complementary;
each instrument has its opportunities, yet they blend. But as
people, Letty and Marcia and Norman and Edwin do not
blend. What the story tells us is that people are alone. What it is
about is caring for other people, or not caring for them, or not
acting on one's caring for them. Edwin postpones getting in

touch with Letty: "He decided to leave it for today and try again tomorrow or whenever he happened to remember it. After all, there was no hurry" (*QA,* 22). It is about people who do not make contact or make it as if subconsciously. "Only connect": but they do not.

The most subtle relationship in the novel is that between Marcia and Norman, two such bristly people in contrast to the mild Letty and the peacemaker Edwin. When Marcia dies it is discovered that she has left Norman her house. It has been the faintest of attractions between them, most delicately, nearly invisibly traced. One must read close. On the surface one of the few signs has been their sharing in the office the tin of Nescafé, the larger "family" size. One of Barbara Pym's favorite poems by Matthew Arnold was one of the Marguerite poems, which begins:

Yes! in the sea of life enisled,
With echoing straits between us thrown,
Dotting the shoreless watery wild,
We mortal millions live *alone.*

The quartet live alone, but across the "echoing straits" Marcia has signaled to Norman. John Updike in the *New Yorker* said that "*Quartet in Autumn* is a marvel of fictional harmonics, a beautifully calm and rounded passage in and out of four isolated individuals as they feebly, fitfully grope toward an ideal solidarity" (February 26, 1979). How tentative the signals are; they are "comic and sad and indefinite"; they transcend the confines of comedy and tragedy into some rarer region.

A Few Green Leaves   If Barbara Pym's next-to-last novel is a quartet, her last one is a coda to her career dal capo al fine. It is a return to the old manner, but muted now; age and illness have laid on their restraining hand. We are back in a village, but

not the timeless little town of *Some Tame Gazelle,* rather a place
where abandoned cars fill the garden of a cottage, where the
vicar hesitates to visit his parishioners and interrupt their ab-
sorption in "the box," where the communal center is not the
church but the "nationalised" doctors' consultation hours: "the
surgery—Mondays and Thursdays" (*FGL,* 3). The decay of
faith is symbolized by the mausoleum in the churchyard where
members of the patrician family, seldom now in residence, were
in the old days buried, and which the vicar, Tom Dagnall, likes
to visit. He is absorbed in the past, in his search for the remains
of the "D.M.V.," the "deserted medieval village" (which is finally found, "a scattering of large stones" [27]), and in his reading of ancient authorities like Anthony à Wood, from whom he
learns that in 1678 a law was enacted that the dead must hence-
forth be buried in woolen shrouds. The villagers in their colorful synthetic clothes, Courtelle and Acrilan, do not remember
the past. They have no sense of tradition; they are shallow and
"televisionized."

The heroine is Emma Howick, an anthropologist living for a
while in Robin Cottage and planning to write a study of some
aspect of the community. After seeing him on a television discussion and writing to him, she resumes a love affair with Dr.
Graham Pettifer, who rents a cottage in the nearby woods to
finish his own anthropological treatise, but who, when he has
done so, returns to his wife in Islington and leaves Emma to
cultivate her growing friendship with Tom. Graham is no loss;
Emma is not alone in finding him "rather a bore."

There are more mentions of characters (living or now dead)
from former novels than there are introductions of new ones
here. Yet there are lively comic types, like Adam Prince, who
writes about food, yet another effete gourmet ("That celery,
cleverly disguised in a rich sauce, *had* it come out of a tin? And

the mayonnaise with the first course, served in an attractive Portuguese pottery bowl, was it *really* home-made?" [*FGL,* 4]). Or Tom's sister Daphne, whose name suits her love of Greece though not her sturdy self, a pathetic, hard-to-live-with woman who ends up not in a sunwashed white Greek villa but in a suburb of Birmingham, with a dog named Bruce and a bossy friend named Heather Blenkinsop. Or a peppy young florist named Terry Skate, who finally gives up his job of decorating the mausoleum because he has lost his faith: "Oh, it's not *books,*" he tells Tom. "It's those talks on the telly" (25).

And there is Miss Lickerish, who lives among hedgehogs and other animals:

> In the next-door cottage Miss Lickerish had not bothered to put on the light at the normal time. She boiled a kettle on the fire and then sat in her chair with a cup of tea at her side and a cat on her knees. But some time during those dark hours the cat left her and sought the warmth of his basket, Miss Lickerish's lap having become strangely chilled. (*FGL,* 28).

The novel is full of deaths, like *Quartet in Autumn,* of mausoleums and the end of things; of the end of traditions, of an era, of a world. There remain a few green leaves, like a wreath laid gracefully on a little monument to their departure.

Miss Pym and the Africans

An anthropologist by definition   In *Jane and Prudence* there is a discussion among village ladies about the marriage of Mildred Lathbury, the heroine of the preceding novel, *Excellent Women:*

> "Who has she married?" asked Miss Morrow.
>
> "An anthropophagist," declared Miss Doggett in an authoritative tone. "He does some kind of scientific work, I believe."
>
> "I thought it meant a cannibal—one who ate human flesh," said Jane in wonder.
>
> "Well, science has made such strides," said Miss Doggett doubtfully. "His name is Mr. Bone."
>
> "That certainly does seem to be a connection," said Jane, laughing, "but perhaps he is an anthro*pologist;* that would be more likely. They don't eat human flesh, as far as I know, though they may study those who do, in Africa and other places."
>
> "Perhaps that is it," said Miss Doggett in a relieved tone.
> (*JP,* 13)

There is ignorance and confusion throughout the novels about what an anthropologist *is,* and what exactly one *does.* Even someone as alert as Sophia Ainger can say of her neighbor, the social anthropologist with a rather anthropological-sounding name, Rupert Stonebird, "I suppose he goes around measuring skulls and that kind of thing" (*UA*, 2). Her sister Penelope, though intent on marrying someone, even an anthropologist, has her reservations: "It seemed a dark mysterious sort of profession, perhaps in a way not quite manly, or not manly in the way she was used to" (7). Rhoda Wellcome, aunt of another marriageable young woman, has similar doubts:

> She liked to think of her niece as being courted by suitable young men, though from what she had heard of them, she rather doubted whether anthropologists could be so regarded. There was something disquieting about all this going out to Africa to study the natives, she felt. (*LA*, 3)

A conversation at a supper party doesn't help her:

> "Now I suppose you Africanists won't want chicken," said Malcolm breezily, the carving implements poised in his hands.
> "What *do* people eat in Africa?" asked Mabel earnestly.
> "The Hadzapi tribe will eat anything that is edible except for the hyena," declared Alaric precisely.
> "Oh, well . . ." Mabel spread out her hands in a hopeless little gesture.
> "The butcher wouldn't offer you hyena anyway," giggled Phyllis.
> "Most African tribes are very fond of meat when they can get it," said Tom.
> "Yes, and many of them relish even putrescent meat," said Alaric solemnly.
> "Do they understand the principles of cooking as we know it?" asked Rhoda.
> "Oh, yes, a good many of them do," said Alaric. "In some very primitive societies, though, they would just fling the unskinned carcase on the fire and hope for the best."
> "Yes, like that film of the Australian aborigines we saw at the Anthropology Club," said Deirdre. "They flung a kangaroo on

the fire and cooked it like that."

"Now who would like some potato salad?" said Rhoda, feeling that there was something a little unappetizing about the
conversation. (*LA*, 12)

Minnie Foresight, the rich little widow in the same novel,
Less than Angels, thinks she quite understands what those who
go out or down to Africa are up to. But Minnie boggles at
some of the "unpleasant details" in a learned journal about initiation ceremonies: "the seclusion of the boys and girls in the
bush—the coming forth—the dancing, and the licence allowed
in certain forms of behaviour . . ." (8).

Suburbanites, rich widows, villagers, everyone is impres-
sively ignorant. Here is Harriet in *Some Tame Gazelle,* convers-
ing with the visiting—visiting from Africa—Bishop of Mbawawa, Theodore Grote:

> "How debased anthropology has become since Frazer's day,"
> sighed the Bishop, "a mere matter of genealogies, meaningless
> definitions and jargon, *words, words, words,* as Hamlet has it;
> lineage, sib, kindred, extended family, ramage—one doesn't
> know where one is. Even the good old term *clan* is suspect."
>
> "What is a sib?" asked Harriet. "It sounds a nice, friendly kind
> of thing, or it might be something to eat, a biscuit, perhaps."
>
> The Bishop shook his head and said nothing, either because
> he did not deign to be associated with present-day anthropo-
> logical terminology or because he did not really know what a
> sib was. (*STG*, 18)

Misprision, ignorance, prejudice, all are matters for joyous confusion concerning the subject of anthropology, which is one of
the staples of the novels.

The uses of anthropology   It is inevitable that it was. Barbara Pym worked nearly thirty years for the International African Institute and came to know about anthropologists and

Africans almost too well. Authors write about what is to hand, and the professional need of anthropologists for observation and objectivity nicely suited her own impartiality. On the other hand their solemnity and jargon suited her comedy. If she laughed at them, she learned from them, though perhaps as much by the force of negative as of positive example. One wonders what kind of novels she might have written had she been a lawyer or physician or merely a lady of private means. One is certain that she would have made ample use of any profession she engaged in, yet it does seem fortunate that the one she chose so suited her own personality and no doubt inspired the flourishing of her special talents.

Her notebooks of the late forties show from the beginning an amused and bemused tolerance of this new world: "Anthropology—I just let it *flow* over me." A little later, in the same notebook: "Essays presented to Professor ——, an anthropologist. Why are they all so obscene?" (MS PYM 40, pp. 7, 23). There are other random entries in the notebooks which show her seizing upon this new life for part of the raw material—the field notes—of her novels. Here is one of her jollier inspirations, in a notebook of the early 1950's: "An anthropologist who had been among the head-shrinkers of the Amazon and whose own head was already beginning to look a little shrunken" (MS PYM 44, p. 19).

Anthropology is everywhere in her books, specifically African anthropology, which was the kind she knew most about. Among the novels, it is central in *Excellent Women, Less than Angels, An Unsuitable Attachment,* and *A Few Green Leaves,* though not, except in *Less than Angels,* as central as the Church. Archaeology, which is a hobby and profession to Sybil Forsyth and her friend Professor Root, takes its place in *A Glass of Blessings.* Africa disappears in *The Sweet Dove Died,* the most brittle of Pym's London novels, surfacing only in an incidental and typical remark of Leonora, who, speaking of her upstairs tenant, the impoverished gentlewoman Miss Foxe, says, "One feels that using paraffin at all is somehow degrading—the sort of thing black people do, upsetting oil heaters and setting the place on fire" (6). In the rest of the novels Africa surfaces ubiquitously, in comic images, similes, titles of pedantic articles, jargon, incidental sly descriptions, names for anthropologists, and most of all in the confrontations between English and African. Mrs. Glaze, Jane's cook in *Jane and Prudence,* complains about a substitute vicar, a Mr. Boultbee:

> "It's tired of Africa, *we* are . . . Six sermons about Africa, we've had. It's more than flesh and blood can stand, madam. I was really shocked at some of their customs." She paused, and then added in a brighter tone, "I've got some nice chops for your supper." (*JP,* 22)

Especially in *A Few Green Leaves* the anthropological zeal for observation, categorization, and card-indexing is triumphant. All the main characters in this novel are in some sense or another anthropologists. Emma Howick, the heroine, is one by profession, and by temperament the inveterate observer; she never stops classifying, whether it is the guests at the parties of the dominant dowager of the village, or rituals like "coffee mornings," "flower festivals," and "other important features of village life," and even the burial ceremony of Miss Lickerish, who had been so devoted to moles and hedgehogs, suggests a paper to be called "Funeral Customs in a Rural Community" (*FGL,* 29). Emma is only mocking herself when she toys with the idea of "A Note on the Significance of the Abandoned Motor-Car in a West Oxfordshire Village" (14).

Emma's mother, Beatrix, analyzes Victorian fiction; the

vicar, Tom Dagnall, studies parish registers; Dr. Shrubsole classifies his geriatric patients, including his mother-in-law; Adam Prince is an inspector of gourmet restaurants for a food magazine: all of them are arranging, ordering, typifying as if their life depended on it. Perhaps it does. They are in a frenzy of reducing human experience to a manageable dimension.

From Harriet and Belinda in *Some Tame Gazelle,* peering out the window to watch the departure of Agatha Hoccleve for a German spa, to Emma Howick in *A Few Green Leaves,* who goes so far as to read the instructions to the milkman left by her neighbor Adam Prince, curiosity ranges from scientific enquiry to—much oftener—the gossipy delights of prying. To be curious is to observe, and to observe can lead, though it sometimes has the opposite effect, to detachment. The most detached of all the anthropologists is Rupert Stonebird, who is left high and dry, if perhaps only for a while, at the end of *An Unsuitable Attachment.* The ending is the wedding of John Challow and Ianthe Broome, the latter of whom Rupert had once courted. His friend Sophia leaves him "to observe the scene. After all, you're used to doing that," she says (23). But his "anthropologist's detachment" preserves him from her irony and from chagrin.

As if eternal vigilance were the price of safety, Barbara Pym's people do not cease to watch one another, even the arch-observers, the anthropologists, themselves undergoing close scrutiny. In *Excellent Women* Mildred and Rocky attend a meeting of a learned society to watch the watchers:

> "Yes, Miss Lathbury, you and I will sit at the back and observe the anthropologists," said Rockingham. "They study mankind and we will study them."
>
> "Well, the society is in many ways a primitive community,"

said Everard, "and offers the same opportunities for field-
work." (*EW,* 4)

The appeal of the quiet life, untroubled because she who
leads it has opted for curiosity, not commitment; for observation, not action: this appeal is a motif in the story of even so
selfish and suffering a heroine as Leonora, as well as to ordinary
bystanders like Rhoda Wellcome.

> And how much more comfortable it sometimes was to observe
> it from a distance, to look down from an upper window, as it
> were, as the anthropologists did. (*LA,* 23)

Or to attractive women like Dulcie Mainwaring:

> It seemed . . . so much safer and more comfortable to live in
> the lives of other people—to observe their joys and sorrows with
> detachment as if one were watching a film or a play. (*NFR,* 12)

The Congo and the Cotswolds   One of the most intellec-
tually interesting aspects of the novels derives from the contrast
between the rites of anthropological Africa and the ceremonies
of the world her characters, and we ourselves, think of as
civilized, in her case the churchy world of flower festival and
jumble sale. It is a basic contrast, between the raw and the re-
fined, between the Congo and the Cotswolds, between the an-
thropophagist, if such there be, and the anthropologist, who
bravely attempts to bridge the two worlds. This juxtaposition
is everywhere. When the sisters Swan and Wellcome see that
their neighbor, Alaric Lydgate, newly back from the field, has
spread his rugs out on the lawn one late afternoon, they are
driven to comment:

> "The morning is really the time to do that . . . Mr. Lydgate
> must realize that he isn't living in the African jungle now. One
> doesn't want to be narrow and suburban, goodness knows, but

if everybody were to beat their rugs in the evening, just think
of the noise!"

"It would be like native drums, I suppose," said Mabel mildly.
(*LA*, 3)

Africa is forever rearing its head, whether in Miss Clovis'
rooms in *Excellent Women*, where Mildred notices "several dark
wooden images, some with fierce and alarming expressions"
(19), or in the jovial Mr. Olatunde in *Quartet in Autumn*. Dulcie Mainwaring considers letting rooms to students: "perhaps
Africans, who would fill the house with gay laughter and cook
yams on their gas-rings" (*NFR*, 25). Africa seems consistently
to stand for some fullness of life, some sensuous richness,
something before or beyond tea caddies and sherry parties.

Yet of course the deeper point is that England *is* Africa.
There's little difference between a fashionable evening in Belgrave Square and the initiation rites that make Minnie Foresight rather uncomfortable. As Tom Mallow realizes:

> It was odd to think that he himself had once been on the
> threshold of that kind of life and that he had thrown it all
> away, as it were, to go out to Africa and study the ways of a
> so-called primitive tribe. For really, when one came to consider
> it, what could be more primitive than the rigid ceremonial of
> launching a debutante on the marriage market? (*LA*, 14)

When Tom revisits his ancestral home in Shropshire, the village
has come to seem another country. He is attending a flower
show:

> The scene reminded him of the African festivals he used to
> attend, observing meticulously how this or that old custom of
> which he had read had died out and been replaced by some
> new and "significant" feature, avoiding in his descriptions the
> least suggestion of vivid or picturesque language, and flatten-

ing out the whole thing until it sounded rather less interesting than a flower show and carnival in a small English market town. . . . Tom felt as if he were observing some aspect of a culture as alien to him as any he had seen in Africa. (*LA*, 16)

Jane Cleveland with her usual penetration summarizes this identity of "primitive" and "civilized" peoples:

> But then, she thought, weren't we all, even the most intelligent of us, like children fearing to go into the dark, no better than primitive peoples with their ancestor cults, the way we went to the cemetery on a Sunday afternoon, bearing bunches of flowers? (*JP*, 11)

Barbara Pym has certainly done more for anthropology than other novelists have, and one is tempted to say more than it has done for itself. She has made Africa come home to England and found that they are the same. Nonetheless she kept in mind the similarities and the differences between the novelist and the anthropologist. The romantic novelist Catherine enters "a large restaurant with a noble foyer"[1] and watches the other patrons:

> They wandered, bewildered, rudderless, in need not only of someone to tell them which of the many separate cafés would supply their immediate material wants, but of a guide to the deeper or higher things of life. While a glance at the menus displayed or a word with an attendant would supply the former, who was to fulfill the latter? The anthropologist, laying bare the structure of society, or the writer of romantic fiction, covering it up? Perhaps neither, Catherine thought. (*LA*, 17)

Late in life Barbara Pym (who was a realistic not a romantic novelist) had come to certain conclusions about the two professions she knew best:

---

1. Probably the Lyons Corner House in Leicester Square.

For many years I worked with anthropologists, when I had the job of preparing their research for publication, and I occasionally regretted that more of them did not turn their undoubted talents to the writing of fiction. Their work often showed many of the qualities that make a novelist—accurate observation, detachment, even sympathy. It only needed a little more imagination, plus the leavening of irony and humor, to turn their accounts into novels.[2]

It is a good description of what her novels are like.

2. "In defence of the novel: Why you shouldn't have to wait until the afternoon," *The Times,* February 22, 1978, p. 18.

Miss Pym and the Comic Muse

Her own tone of voice How pleasant to meet Miss Pym. Inevitably one would meet her at tea. It would probably be China tea. She would talk about people more than about politics, about movies rather than metaphysics, about books not about God. Her conversation would be well-bred, urbane, ironic, with a hovering sense of the absurd; it would never be contentious or dogmatic or impertinent. In conversation the worst sort of person of all is the one who won't listen to what you say, who is eagerly full of herself, relentlessly autobiographical and opinionated. But Miss Pym would be the opposite of all this; she would never hold forth. Even in her very personal diaries, she didn't lay much claim to ego.

Now we cannot meet her in person; we never did and we never will; we can only meet her in the long teatime of her books. Teatime is not dinner; it is a more limited occasion, a minor not a major one. The heat of the sun has waned, and night isn't yet upon us. If it begins to get dark during tea, we will draw the curtains against the outside, and continue talking for a little while.

She never talks too much in her books. In what she says and how she says it there is a certain reserve: no flights of fancy, no passionate yearnings; no open artifice or architectural richnesses or any, as Dr. Johnson called them, "sesquipedalian ponderosities." It is the opposite of adjectival—she preferred adverbs; it is uncluttered and clear and fluent, with many subject-verb declarative sentences, smoothly varied as to phrases and clauses. It's rhythmic without being musical. She reads very well aloud. Her style is not poetic; it is prose exactly suited to her subject.

Specifically it is an English style, one where lucidity is the mean, banality the deficiency, and floridity the excess. There are, it is true, ripe and rich English stylists, just as there are barebones American stylists (of whom Hemingway is often the chosen, I think mistaken, example), but if one can generalize, Evelyn Waugh is an English stylist and William Faulkner an American. Barbara Pym belongs in the English tradition of the statement made simply and surely. Her style does not have echoes; we always know what she is saying.

But there are bare bones in the English and French styles of Beckett, bones stripped as if with acid, and her style can scarcely be said to be like his. One difference is that Beckett's people are talking to themselves, in a grave, while Barbara Pym's are talking to us, at teatime. She intends to communicate, and again style and subject become the same, because what happens in her novels except the efforts of her characters to communicate? Beckett's Molloy and Malone talk to themselves because there is no one to talk to, and even they themselves may not be there. The narrative voice in Beckett and in much of the "intellectual" novel of our time is "solipsistic," "self-reflexive," glassed in by technique; it is self-absorbed and contained and confined to notation, not explanation. This voice must talk to itself because it is uncertain that there is any other self out there to talk to. There is no "community of belief," and there hasn't been since Matthew Arnold said there wasn't. There are no agreed-on anythings, of morals or standards or creeds.

The quiet assumption of Barbara Pym is that there is someone to talk to. It is one aspect of her nostalgic appeal. Her great
predecessors in the English novel addressed their readers con-
fidently, whether George Eliot or Dickens or Charlotte Brontë
("Reader, I married him"). There was not only someone to ad-
dress, there was someone to educate and sermonize. Today a
reader's expectations are still based upon the congeniality of
those old writers and their moral intimacy. Barbara Pym did
not put on the robes of preacher, but she could speak with us,
not just with herself, and did. We are spared the melodrama and
sentimentality of the Victorians; her novels have thinner di-
mensions than theirs; but she believed like them that a story-
teller should entertain.

Her tone of voice is immediately recognizable. Just as one
reads here or there about a real person who is "like someone in
Barbara Pym," one begins to hear her now and then even in the
chance remarks of strangers. Her style becomes more like itself,
I believe, as the novels progress; by the time of her fourth published novel, *Less than Angels,* she is in exuberant command.
If it is not too odd a comparison one could say that, just as a
certain painting by Goya is more like Goya than other Goya
paintings, she is at her most characteristic in *Less than Angels.*
One feels the joy in her voice, that of an artist entirely in command of her instrument.

Yet the voice has its complexities. In fact it is a double voice,
one above that presents and one beneath that comments. The
distance between the two is the distance of irony. Hence her
variety of point of view. Adroitly she slips from one person's
outlook to another's, though one always hears her own unmistakable tone.

At times a character's manner of expression and viewpoint are
so like her own that the gap between them narrows or disap-

pears. Most of her heroines have her own ironic intelligence. When Catherine Oliphant regards the world and its inhabitants, it is often Barbara Pym herself we hear. All the heroines to greater or lesser degree comment like Barbara Pym herself. Emma in *A Few Green Leaves* may be the closest; Leonora, in *The Sweet Dove Died,* at the farthest remove. But Catherine and Wilmet and Mildred and even Belinda can become Barbara. Minor characters, even men, can have their moments of right perspicacity.

How do we judge their accuracy; how do we know when their perceptions are hers and meant to be ours? The answer to the question is that the problem doesn't exist. Just as we depend on our intuitions in life, we simply *know* when Belinda is being too mild or Prudence silly or Wilmet obtuse. The author has both educed and directed our native insight. It is an easy game, to know that Ned is false and Tom Dagnall is true. With the heroines it is a subtler yet sure pursuit, to determine that Catherine is too fey and Dulcie too put-upon, thus to discern when they are Barbara and thus are ourselves.

Adverbs and epigrams   To talk about comedy is sometimes to take the fun out of it, as when one has to explain a joke, but if there are enough examples, one can say, since comedy is concerned with clichés, that they sweeten the pill. Most theories of comedy, Meredith's or Bergson's or Freud's, are quite depressing; comedy and literary theory seem to be a contradiction in terms. There is much more written about tragedy than about comedy, either because the former is more self-important or more germane to our experience, or because the latter is like quicksilver, or a butterfly, or a soap bubble, too rapid and buoyant to be captured or pinned down.

Incongruity, irrelevance, inconsequence, and enlargement are some terms, though many others might do as well, which might help to explain the means by which Barbara Pym makes us laugh. By enlargement, to take the last first, I mean a moment when the mundane or trivial is suddenly amplified. Here is Fabian Driver in *Jane and Prudence,* when Miss Doggett discovers that there is "something between" him and Jessie Morrow:

> He supposed that the occasion was one which called for a drink; indeed, in his life there was hardly any occasion which did not. (*JP,* 19)

Or when a flat description of the vicarage in *An Unsuitable Attachment* comes awake:

> The vicarage had been built to match the church and the style of the rooms had not yet, and perhaps never would, become fashionable again. (*UA,* 1)

Irrelevance is named as such when Belinda is speaking of her old University Library:

> "Old Mr. Lydgate is in charge now, but I should think he is hardly up to the work really, though," she added irrelevantly, "he had some very interesting experiences in Ethiopia." (*STG,* 12)

Or it could be termed inconsequence, or incongruity. In *Excellent Women* Mildred recalls a lunch with William Caldicote earlier in the day:

> I shouldn't have gossiped to William in that naughty way, and in Lent, too. (*EW,* 8)

Barbara Pym has several ways of undercutting her characters. They are most frequent in *Some Tame Gazelle,* her most playful book:

> "*Dies Irae,*" he [the Archdeacon] continued, lingering on the words with enjoyment. (*STG,* 10)

Or Dr. Parnell:

> "Sloth and lethargy," said Dr. Parnell, with relish. (*STG,* 9)

Or Harriet, speaking of her sister's illness:

> "She had weak tea and dry toast for breakfast," said Harriet confidentially, "and then she asked for the *Oxford Book of Victorian Verse.*" (*STG,* 17)

There is more of the simply absurd in *Some Tame Gazelle* than in any of the other novels, as at Belinda and Harriet's dinner party:

> The curate leaned forward eagerly. "It is wonderful what things animals and even insects can be made to do if they are trained with kindness," he said, his face aglow with interest.
>
> Everyone agreed with this very just remark. Dr. Parnell even went so far as to observe that it was also true of people. (*STG,* 11)

Mr. Donne is the most foolish curate in the world. Early in her acquaintance with him Harriet urges him not to enter the Mission Field—"you aren't *commanded* to go by your bishop, are you?"

> "Oh no, it is a personal matter. The call comes from within, as it were," explained Mr. Donne, rather red in the face. (*STG,* 5)

Mr. Donne has, as it were, the dimmest abilities of articulation. In the same conversation Harriet is dissatisfied to learn that "a female Don" is knitting socks for her protégé:

> "Her name's Olivia Berridge and she's awfully nice," said the curate in a kind of burst. (*STG,* 5)

As some of the examples have already shown, adverbs often accompany statements to underscore how fatuous they are. When the Archdeacon thinks of Gray's *Elegy,* and he is dangerously given to literature, he speaks "affectedly" (*STG,* 5, 6), while his wife, who has much to put up with, holds her own by smiling at him or his devoted Belinda "indulgently" or "complacently" (6). A favorite adverb is "stoutly," often added to the utterances of that stout lady Harriet.

To snort is to express contempt stoutly, and Harriet likes to snort, as when she hears of the Archdeacon's "affectedly" melancholy stroll in a churchyard (*STG,* 8), and other stout ladies similarly indulge themselves: Edith Liversidge in the same novel, Sister Blatt several times in *Excellent Women,* and Esther Clovis, famous for snorting, throughout both *Excellent Women* and *Less than Angels.* These women have in common a tendency to derision, and snorting is their bold, even abandoned, way of expressing it.

It could not be called a polite usage, but the reign of propriety is precarious everywhere. The natural shock-effect of the outré and the obscene, which is or isn't humorous depending on the reader, is more evident in *Quartet in Autumn* than in the earlier novels. Letty is visiting her friend Marjorie in the country and helping to entertain Marjorie's soon-to-be fiancé, Father Lydell, at dinner:

> "Do you find the country is doing you good?" Letty asked.
> "I've had diarrhoea all this week," came the disconcerting reply. (*QA,* 5)

It is Letty, a gentle woman, who is most assaulted: "Fuck off!" she hears a woman shouting on an Underground platform (2); less comprehending is another of the quartet, Marcia, who sees scrawled on the wall of, again, an Underground station, "KILL ASIAN SHIT" (2). In the final novel, *A Few Green Leaves,* there is an odd eruption at a dinner party:

> "Do you see many foxes here?" Isobel asked.

> "Oh yes—and you can find their traces in the woods," said
> Daphne eagerly. "Did you know that a fox's dung is grey and
> pointed at both ends?"
> Nobody did know and there was a brief silence. It seemed diffi-
> cult to follow such a stunning piece of information. (*FGL*, 12)

Of course there is more scatology in a paragraph of some modern novels than there is in the twelve of these, but, in my opinion, it jars with the usual equable tone.

Without disturbing the tone an occasional witticism summarizes a sharp perception. They may be too long to be called epigrams, yet they have that sort of succinct or cynical wit. Belinda
is visited by the Archdeacon, who has a houseguest he dislikes,
the Bishop of Mbawawa:

> It was at once evident that he was in a good temper, which
> Belinda thought rather surprising, although there was a certain
> relish in disliking somebody, she supposed, which might ac-
> count for it. (*STG*, 16)

On the first page of the next novel, *Excellent Women,* Mildred
Lathbury tells us about herself:

> I suppose an unmarried woman just over thirty, who lives
> alone and has no apparent ties, must expect to find herself in
> volved or interested in other people's business, and if she is
> also a clergyman's daughter then one might really say that
> there is no hope for her. (*EW*, 1)

But it is the flow of dramatized experience, not its crystalliza-
tion into epigram, that is the rule. It is dialogue, not discussion; showing, not telling.

Far more common than epigram is another literary, but never
too literary, usage—that of similes. These are as close as Barbara Pym's craft comes to display, but their humor preserves
them from ostentation. It is true that once in a while they are

meant seriously, as when we are told about Sophia's husband in
An Unsuitable Attachment:

> . . . Mark's eyes, which were also blue, but with that remote
> expression sometimes found in the eyes of sailors or explorers.
> (*UA*, 1)

Or, more powerfully, when Catherine, who writes for women's
magazines, reflects at the beginning of *Less than Angels:*

> . . . life itself was sometimes too strong and raw and must be
> made palatable by fancy, as tough meat may be made tender by
> mincing. (*LA*, 1)

Usually, however, they are comic. In the same novel Deirdre has
met Tom Mallow and begun to deplore her businessman boy-
friend Bernard:

> Bernard's dullness seemed to have a positive quality about it so
> that it was almost a physical agony, like the dentist's drill press-
> ing on a sensitive tooth. (*LA*, 4)

Again in *Less than Angels*, Professor Felix Byron Mainwaring
gives his judicious estimate of Tom:

> "Mallow is very sound, you know," he added, as if Tom were a
> fruit suitable for bottling. (*LA*, 10)

Some Tame Gazelle, the first and most "literary" of the novels,
has the most similes. Twice Edith Liversidge bears the brunt;
we are told about her "old-fashioned grey costume,"

> whose unfashionably narrow shoulders combined with Edith's
> broad hips made her look rather like a lighthouse. (*STG*, 2)

Again Miss Liversidge, this time in action:

> [She] stumped off in search of her relative, Miss Aspinall, call-
> ing her as if she were a dog, "Connie! Connie! Come along!

Time to go home to lunch." (*STG*, 2)

But there are these comparisons throughout. One of the best is in *An Unsuitable Attachment,* when Ianthe is watching her uncle, the Reverend Randolph Burdon, at lunch:

> He carved the saddle of mutton savagely, as if he were rending his parishioners. (*UA*, 8)

Similes brighten prose, just as clichés deaden it. Barbara Pym does not write in clichés, she writes about them, worn-out attitudes and thoughtless or programmed conduct. Just as similes are an ancient poetic device, the usage of clichés to satirize is an old one, especially in the drama. A character who speaks in clichés is too unintelligent or lazy or even frightened to speak the truth; they are conservative and comfortable, and it would be interesting to know what proportion of our daily speech is composed of them. Jane in *Jane and Prudence* sounds odd because she is incapable of them, and Marcia is capable of little else—Marcia, who thinks she keeps even the cat's dishes in her dirty house "spotlessly clean" and who comforted herself at the time of Snowy's death with the platitude "In the midst of life we are in death" (*QA*, 16).

Clichés are so pervasive in these novels that quotation could be endless. One extended example will serve. Gerald Beamish is the brother of Mary Beamish in *A Glass of Blessings,* and he is speaking to Wilmet at his sister's wedding to Father Marius Ransome:

> "So I was right after all," chuckled Gerald Beamish, "and they talk about *woman's* intuition! It didn't take *me* long to see which way the wind was blowing. Mary was keen on this fellow, but he had ideas about celibacy and all that kind of thing, as these young parsons sometimes do have; so off she goes into a convent and he very soon realizes he's missed the boat.

Quite a clever move of Mary's that—I'd never have thought
her capable of such cunning. It only shows we should never
underestimate women, doesn't it?"

"Men should never do that," I agreed. "But of course that
wasn't the reason why Mary went into the convent. She was
really convinced that it was the best life for her."

"But a good looking husband's even better, eh?" he chuckled,
stuffing a last bit of cake into his mouth. "Well, I've had enough of
this bun fight now—only came to see Mary, really—family
support and all that, you know. I suppose one can slip away
quite easily?" (*GB*, 23)

Here it all is, from worn-out metaphors like "missing the boat"
to the verbal inertia of "and all that" and "and all that kind of
thing." It is quite a demolition job performed on this chuckling
chauvinist, and of course he does it all himself. Wedding cake
goes into his mouth, and nothing but toads come out. It is a
relentless and moral passage, and at the same time very funny.

To list clichés and similes, adverbs and absurdities, is like visiting rooms in a museum where armor and weapons are displayed which, though grim and well-polished, really suggest
very little of the battles where people employed them, and
fought. Despite a well-stocked arsenal the battles of Barbara
Pym are never lethal. Skirmishes only, which dissolve into
laughter; pleasant interludes.

Humors The decayed gentlewoman, the finicky gourmet,
the mannish tweedy spinster, the mild and ineffectual clergyman are characters it is easy to summarize. They are types, humors, embodiments of a generalization, a sort of psychological shorthand. If they are simpler than we know people are,
they are more manageable, nor are they so far from our experience that they can't strike home. They have been with us since
Theophrastus, or before; they survive today not as the old me-

dievalist biles and blood and phlegm but in popular, more or less remotely Freudian jargon like "narcissist," "father figure," "dominatrix," or such.

They are to personality what clichés are to language, but the difference is that, grounded on some fundamental human attributes, they retain their vitality, while clichés have long since lost theirs and are in fact dead. The characters of Dickens that we joyfully remember are the humorous characters; most of the heroes and heroines we wish we could forget. Uriah Heep will wring his hands forever, and Mrs. Micawber never will desert Mr. Micawber, her spouse.

In Barbara Pym there are no villains, no heroes—though perhaps a heroine or two. Both stock figures and leading personages have obsessions, frequently inanimate or subspecies, like Mrs. Forbes with her stuffed eagle, Miss Liverish with her hedgehogs, Marcia with milkbottles, Tom Dagnall with the D.M.V. In *Some Tame Gazelle,* a gentle Jonsonian revel, everyone has an idée fixe or two. With Harriet it's curates; with Belinda, the Archdeacon; with the Archdeacon, himself; with Count Bianco, both Harriet and his dead friend John Akenside; with both Dr. Parnell and Miss Liversidge, "sanitary facilities." Obsession can become poignant and complex even though retaining comic overtones in some of the heroines; one thinks of Sophia and motherhood, Leonora and exquisiteness. The obsessed ones are bound to a wheel, of compulsive preference or mania, and it's a good thing they are, or they might fly off in all directions. It is especially young women, and Barbara Pym is tender with them, who are bound to love, who grope for it in their awkward and callow and appealing way—Deirdre Swan in *Less than Angels,* or Flora in *Jane and Prudence,* or Phoebe in *The Sweet Dove Died.*

There is no one in the novels with whom we can wholly

identify because Barbara Pym, with no matter what amount of compassion, is detached from every one of them, and also because she is her own chief character. It is her voice which we hear, impartial, curious, and amused; and by which every deviation from normality, whatever normality is, is sanely—not judged, but observed.[1]

She was so curious about people that even when she created a comedy of situation it's a comedy of character. This is the case when Digby and Mark, budding and impoverished anthropologists in *Less than Angels,* boldly take those blown roses Miss Lydgate and Miss Clovis to lunch. (Digby thinks resentfully that "they looked like the kind of women who would eat red meat.") The two students have little over a pound between them. While the elder anthropologists make out a hearty meal, Mark becomes (though "not exactly," he admits) a vegetarian and selects "Macaroni Cheese (1/9)"; Digby chooses "Braised Tripe (2/—)," and both declare that for dessert they are "passionately fond of Jelly (6d)." But after these sacrifices Miss Clovis grabs the bill: "I shouldn't dream of letting you pay," she said indignantly. "This is to be our treat, isn't it, Gertrude?" (*LA*, 8)

Later Mark and Digby are characters in another situation comedy along with two young women, the four of them "candidates for the Foresight research grants." This is Chapters 18 and 19 in *Less than Angels;* it would make a good one-act play, a farce, in itself. The four cynical, ambitious, and amusing students are the victims of a weekend at the country house of Professor Felix Mainwaring, who plies them with heavy repasts, saturnine courtesies, and a player piano. His purpose is to

---

1. I exclude *An Academic Question,* which is insufficiently distanced, from these generalizations.

judge them; only two research grants are available. The ordeal and the weekend are ended with the sudden discovery that Father Gemini, another anthropologist, has captured the attention and money of Minnie Foresight ("Gemini—twins—there is something two-faced even about his name," declares Miss Lydgate when she learns [20]). There will be no grants, and the four students return to London ebullient, empty-handed, and more cynical than ever.

Here again it's people more than plot. Her interest in people is Barbara Pym's own obsession. Her skill is to make us share it.

Miss Pym and Men and Women

Basics Barbara Pym's novels concern the relationships between men and women. Witty, subtle, gracious, and unadorned as her style is, beneath it or behind it there is the raw material of how the sexes comport themselves with each other. They need each other; to put it rawly, it's a question of biology and the continuation of the race. Her characters do not seem very animal in their appetites, but the appetites are indeed there. If it is true that all power is sexual in nature, in these novels men obviously are the power figures: yet women, of whom even the most excellent have their drives and their strategies, can succeed in manipulating the slower-witted males. Perhaps some of the innumerable put-downs by women of men, and in fact of themselves, are a reaction of distaste at having to be manipulative. They become weary of being clever.

Shaw seems to have believed that a woman would stoop to any maneuver to get the man she needed, even a man she laughed at or despised, because she was the vessel of the "Life Force," that energy that insured the propagation of the species. Ann Whitefield in *Man and Superman* is the most striking embodiment of it; her methods of capturing a mate aren't much different from those of Jessie Morrow and Prudence Bates in *Jane and Prudence*. Despite or because of the need, women and men really do not like each other in the world of Barbara Pym.

A woman may dote on a man, want to mother him, bed him, feed him, but rarely is the relationship quite courteous—equal, affectionate, and communicating. Pym's men, I should add, do not dote on women; they prefer to dote on themselves; they are a narcissistic crew. Barbara Pym shows us no more than a handful of sophisticated and satisfactory male/female alliances; the few I can think of seem, surprisingly, mostly between older people like Sybil Forsyth and Professor Root in *A Glass of Blessings* or Sophia Ainger's aunt and her lover, a scholarly old Italian, in *An Unsuitable Attachment.*

There are many examples, however, of friendships between women, where sex barely enters in, if at all; it is only a strand in the relationship. We do not learn much about male friendships; males seem to know each other, and can dislike each other, but liking very seldom enters in. Digby Fox and his fellow-student Mark Penfold do seem to get along pretty well together in *Less than Angels.*

We see more of gay male friendships than we do of straight male friendships. The outlook is a little muddied here because Barbara Pym felt a personal attraction toward gay men and sometimes created gay types in straight costumes, so to speak, like Rocky Napier in *Excellent Women.* Another factor that can mislead an American reader is that English gentlemen can be gentle and American male ideals tend to be more robust (with machismo aspirations at the lunatic male fringe); it can be difficult in Rocky/Rambo land to distinguish effeteness from gentility.

To discuss the various forms relationships between women and men assume in these novels, I will first comment on marriage and the other accommodations that women make, such as excellent spinsterhood or the attempts at a career of liberated independence. As for men, I think the clergy deserve separate

consideration because there are so many of them. Male homo-
sexuals are also a subject of their own for the same reason. Last,
I'll attempt a compilation of the opinions of men about women,
women about women, and, especially, women about men.

Marriage   ". . . ridiculous, really."

"Well, in a way, that's what it is, isn't it, the relationship between men and women," says Beatrix Howick, agreeing with
her daughter Emma, who is the heroine of the last novel, *A Few
Green Leaves* (12). Beatrix is not quite a qualified judge, since
her own marriage was only a "short experience," and since,
though she "did not like to think of herself as a conventional
match-making mother" (12), she smartly maneuvers Emma in
the direction of the vicar, Tom Dagnall.

Marriage maneuvers occupy these novels. At the same time,
the picture of the wedded state, men being what they are, is
scarcely the happy fulfillment it is in the Victorian novel, Beatrix's specialty. "But wasn't that what so many marriages were—
finding a person boring and irritating and yet loving him?" Jane
asks herself in *Jane and Prudence* (20). Jane is the best authority:
she remembers "the grey and fawn couples one saw so often in
hotel lounges, hardly distinguishable, men from women, in
their dimness" (20), and, when her husband Nicholas has once
again beamed at her over his spectacles, she thinks, "Beamy and
beaky, mild, kindly looks and spectacles . . . whether in the
Church or in the Senior Common Room of some Oxford College—it's all one really" (13). Equally prosaic is the romantic
Prudence's friend Eleanor, in her tweed skirt and lisle stockings: "One had to settle down sooner or later into the comfortable spinster or the contented or bored wife" (21).

Contentment is rarer than boredom. Other conditions exist.
Helena and Rocky Napier in *Excellent Women* are a quarrelsome
pair, especially when she sets a hot saucepan on his walnut

table, and the Archdeacon and Agatha Hoccleve in *Some Tame Gazelle* live in a state of skirmish. Elsewhere marriage dwindles into routine, even with a pair who seem as well-adjusted as Wilmet and Rodney in *A Glass of Blessings;* it has become a matter of his giving her money on her birthday or at Christmas a substantial check (though "generally some small token as well," like a pair of pearl earrings [8]).

It seems a matter of "the letter killeth." Sophia Ainger in *An Unsuitable Attachment* loves both her cat Faustina and her husband Mark, in that order, but a much more romantic union is suggested by her aunt's long liaison with an Italian professor (an expert in the "Konso funeral statues" of Ethiopia). Wilmet's sixty-nine-year-old mother-in-law Sybil marries her friend, the archaeologist Professor Root, near the end of *A Glass of Blessings:* perhaps it is only the elderly, calm of mind but with yet a little passion unspent, who achieve a union unmarred by boredom and habit.

Marriage is a project or a promise, seldom a happy ending. Of marriages that occur between novels, such as Mildred's to Everard, Catherine's to Alaric, or Dulcie's to Aylwin, we learn nothing. Perhaps we do not want to know.

Excellent women   An alternative to marriage for a woman is a single life of piety and good works. The cleaning woman of that excellent woman Mildred Lathbury, Mrs. Morris, says, "It's not natural for a woman to live alone, without a husband" (18). But Mildred thinks, "It was not the excellent women who got married but people like Allegra Gray, who was no good at sewing, and Helena Napier, who left all the washing up" (18). Mildred does it for them, both sewing and washing up. When she tells Rocky, Helena's husband, about "the many rejected ones who lived in lonely bed-sitting-rooms with nobody to talk to them or prepare meals for them," Rocky says callously, "They could always wash stockings or something" (7).

It is an excellent thing in women to do good in their church, to engage in volunteer work in a society for distressed gentle-women, to look after the unattached men who need looking after, which is most of them. Belinda in *Some Tame Gazelle* feels that she is "dowdy and insignificant, one of the many thousand respectable middle-aged spinsters, the backbones or busybod-ies of countless parishes throughout the country" (16). Dulcie Mainwaring says that ". . . perhaps women enjoy that most of all—to feel that they're needed and doing good," but later on: "It was sad, she thought, how women longed to be needed and useful and how seldom most of them really were" (*NFR*, 11).

However, Belinda and Mildred and Dulcie are characters from novels published in the fifties. Times have changed; women are at least a little freer in *A Few Green Leaves* (1980); at least some of them are. In the England of the eighties, if Mil-dreds exist, there must be far fewer of them; they must be con-scious that other women, younger women especially, are satis-fied with the role neither of Martha nor of Mary. They must occasionally feel rather eccentric. But England harbors eccen-trics, and probably the Mildreds will continue to exist unless even more fundamental changes than those since the war occur in England. It will not, of course, be the excellent women who lead the revolution.

Toward liberation   What is a spinster's alternative to lead-ing an excellent life? At least half of Barbara Pym's unmarried heroines have a private income, an unlikely high proportion; for the married heroines, the husband provides; there is the oc-casional writer, office worker, anthropologist. We know that in the Victorian age scarcely any occupations were open to respect-able women besides those of governess, teacher, and compan-ion, and the women of Barbara Pym have only a significantly few other professions to choose from. Somewhat anachronistically or even nostalgically her women rarely carve careers for themselves, instead depending on their fathers' endeavors or their husbands' enterprise. It does not help their egos, and men's need no assistance.

There are independent types scattered through the novels like Gertrude Lydgate, mistress of phonemes, and her friend Esther Clovis, who advises Helena Napier:

> "You will do better work without your husband," said Miss Clovis. "You will now be able to devote your whole life to the study of matrilineal kin-groups." (*EW*, 19)

Other confident, brusque women are Dora Caldicote (schoolmistress) in *Excellent Women* and Eleanor Hitchens (tweed skirt, lisle stockings; employed at a Ministry) in *Jane and Prudence*. They are not presented as a very appealing alternative.

If these and others like them in the novels are women who have espoused liberation, they are far from conscious spokespersons for it. The attitude of Barbara Pym toward female emancipation is as deft and nondogmatic as her attitudes everywhere. It must have concerned her, yet she does not deal with it explicitly; even in her private writings there is only the rare relevant entry:

> Iris has rejected her husband—used him and then passed on. So often one sees men doing this it is heartening, encouraging and refreshing when a woman does.[1]

The novels are replete with examples of men using women, but generalizations about this sort of traditional injustice or about women's rebellion against it are hard to find. Catherine

---

1. This is a note for *An Academic Question*, which she was working on at this time; MS PYM, p. 4.

in *Less than Angels* is intelligently noncommital:

> "That's what seems wrong with so many relationships now, the
> women feeling that *they* are the strong ones and that men
> couldn't get on without them. In the olden days," she smiled
> at the phrase, "it was quite different—or so we always imag-
> ine. Or were women more diplomatic then?" (*LA*, 9)

In *No Fond Return of Love* Viola Dace's interest in her suitor,
Mr. Bill Sedge the Austrian emigré, is also ambiguous:

> . . . as she had said to Dulcie, he did make her feel that she
> was a *woman,* and that—in these pushing, jostling days of the
> so-called equality of the sexes—was a great deal. (*NFR*, 17)

The novel most relevant to the question of women's liberation is *An Unsuitable Attachment.* All three central women in
this novel, written in the early sixties and thus a later work than
either of the two just cited, are, surprisingly, rather reactionary.
Ianthe Broome's thoughts are interesting for their sexual imag-
ery as well as their atavistic outlook.

> On the crowded train a man gave up his seat to Ianthe and
> she accepted it gracefully. She expected courtesy from men
> and often received it. It was as if they realised that she was not
> for the rough and tumble of this world, like the aggressive
> women with shaggy hair styles who pushed their way through
> life thrusting their hard shopping baskets at defenseless men.
> (*UA*, 2)

When her friend Sophia visits Ianthe, who is ill, she finds their
neighbor Rupert Stonebird filling Ianthe's hot water bottle
(another suggestive metaphor):

> "So I see," said Sophia, unable to keep a note of indignation
> out of her tone, for it was most disquieting that the man she
> intended for her sister's husband should be discovered filling

the hot water bottle of another woman. Besides, filling hot water bottles was not man's work—fetching coal, sawing wood, even opening a bottle of wine would have been suitable occupations for Rupert to be discovered in, but not this.

"You should have taken the cover off before you filled it," she went on, taking the bottle, almost snatching it, out of Rupert's hand. "Look, it's all wet." (*UA*, 9)

Yet both Ianthe and Sophia are women in their thirties and clergy-bred or wed. One might expect Sophia's young sister Penelope to be more advanced. But she is not. During supper at the vicarage she is beginning to be interested in Rupert:

Penelope felt rather bored and irritated and began to speculate on whether Rupert had a car and would offer to run her home. She laid great stress on these little courtesies, the formal acts of politeness that women in their emancipated state seemed to be in danger of losing. (*UA*, 3)

Later Penelope agrees with Ianthe that "a wife should consider her husband's work before her own happiness," and Barbara Pym comments with open irony, "like many modern young women she had the right old-fashioned ideas about men and their work" (5).

Feminists can make a feminist of Barbara Pym only rarely by her statements in her own voice; they will have to rely on her dramatizations, not her explications. The former are countless, of women's subservient role in home, office, church, everywhere. Yet no matter how shrewd, they are a show of the state of things, not a shout against them. Certainly there are women who hold their own in the battle with men, who lead many a successful attack, who even triumph, like Jessie Morrow in *Jane and Prudence*. That the more passive and mild-mannered (like Mildred in *Excellent Women* or Dulcie in *No Fond Return of*

Love) have their own victories is another point. The issue of assertiveness versus diplomacy is a stalemate; to decide it, to award the palm, would be to diminish Barbara Pym's tolerant shrewdness.

No man's land   To turn from women and their accommodations, to men, who do not have to make them, one should say first that there are women, and there are men, and there are clergymen. In *Quartet in Autumn,* Letty questions this distinction:

> Letty had an old-fashioned respect for the clergy which seemed outmoded in the seventies, when it was continually being brought home to her that in many ways they were just like other men, or even more so. (*QA,* 23)

But Letty's opinion is a lone one. Dora Caldicote characteristically, if not invariably, maintains that ". . . clergymen didn't count as men and therefore couldn't be expected to have human feelings" (*EW,* 11). Her friend Mildred admits that clergymen are not the same, though after all, they are "human beings, and might be supposed to share the weaknesses of normal men" (11). Mildred's vicar, Father Malory, rather inadequately attempting to distemper a room, is also dubious:

> "I suppose I am not to be considered a normal man," said Julian, taking off his yellow-streaked cassock and draping it over the step-ladder, "and yet I do have these manly feelings." (*EW,* 5)

Julian's engagement to the glamorous Allegra Gray is short-lived. What would their marriage have been like? In *A Few Green Leaves* Daphne Dagnall has made a home for her brother after his wife's death:

> If it hadn't been for her doing this, Tom might have married again, probably would have done, seeing the way women went

after the clergy. Had she protected him from a grisly fate or
stood in the way of his happiness? She would never know.
(*FGL*, 17)

Why do women "go after" clergymen, if Daphne is right? It
may be because they might be expected to be gentler and less
egotistical than "normal" men. Yet Ianthe in *An Unsuitable Attachment* is happy that her fiancé John is "different from the
men she had been seeing . . . all her life":

> . . . different from Mark Ainger and Basil Branche, from
> Edwin Pettigrew and Rupert Stonebird, and from all the ranks
> of clergymen and schoolmasters stretching back into the past
> like pale imitations of men, it now seemed. (*UA*, 18)

Ianthe's friend Sophia had hoped that Ianthe would not marry,
would become one of the excellent women: who might be
called "pale imitations of women" just as clergymen are "pale
imitations of men."

Male bondings   However, clergymen are still men who are
interested in women. Sybil Forsyth in *A Glass of Blessings* comments on the church scandals which the gutter press likes to
headline, and which concern men who are interested in other
men (1). One is happy to report, for the sake of that institution, that in Barbara Pym's church there are no homosexual
clergymen. There are languid Firbankian types like Father Basil
Branche in *An Unsuitable Attachment* or Father David Lydell in
Quartet in Autumn, but we are spared psychosexual analysis of
them. And of the lay figures, so to speak, abounding in the pur-
lieus of the church—minor servers, masters of ceremony, and
the like, who join the curates for an evening's innocent fun at a
performance of the Crazy Gang (*GB*, 6).

As early as *Excellent Women*, Mildred is remembering at Oxford "a willowy young man of a type that does not look as if it

would marry" (13). They need not be willowy. William Caldicote, Mildred's friend, who was also the friend of the young
man at Oxford, enjoys his food too much to have remained so.
Repressed, or suppressed, or nothing at all, William is as partial
to fine wine as he is opposed to marriage:

> "But my dear Mildred, *you* mustn't marry," he was saying in-
> dignantly. "Life is disturbing enough as it is without these
> alarming suggestions. I always think of you as being so very
> balanced and sensible, such an excellent woman. I do hope
> you're *not* thinking of getting married?" (*EW*, 8)

James, in *The Sweet Dove Died*, may be too young to have
settled in a sexual direction. Veering actively between a male
lover and a female lover, he seems most at home with the asex-
ual heroine Leonora. But Piers Longridge of *A Glass of Blessings*
has found his harbor. The only major homosexual figure in the
novels, he is more attractive in every respect than the William
Caldicotes and Mervyn Cantrells. Just as Ned in *The Sweet Dove
Died* would be hideous whatever he was, Piers is likable; yet,
like William who wants Mildred to remain an excellent woman,
Piers wants Wilmet to be "cool and dignified" (*GB*, 17); he is in
love, as much as he could be in love with a woman, with her
image, and doesn't want enthusiasm or romance to blur its
edges:

> "Dear Wilmet, so deliciously in character! Don't ever try to
> make yourself any different." (*GB*, 17)

A "daunting suggestion," and in a way insulting; an image cannot respond, and Wilmet is a woman, not a statue.

There is nothing intimidating about Piers' lover Keith. A
common youth from Leicester who models for knitwear pho-
tographs, and whom Wilmet finds "impossible to dislike" (*GB*,

17), he is busily occupied with detergents and whether or not curtains are lined. He is gushy, banal, polite, beautiful, boring, and harmless. The florist Terry in *A Few Green Leaves,* a novel which is full of echoes, recalls Keith. He is to decorate Tom's church: "Being a church person myself I got the job, my friend being agnostic . . . You'd have to be a believer, wouldn't you, to do a mausoleum?" (9).

By far the funniest of the gay crowd is the gourmet cook at the vicarage of St. Luke's, Wilfrid J. Bason, in *A Glass of Blessings.* He is the Wilf of the egg-shaped head, who steals a Fabergé egg, and who is later to grow an egg-shaped beard. Wilmet has learned of the theft, and encounters him in a grocery store:

> "Father Bode *will* have his cornflakes," said Mr. Bason, seizing a giant packet of Kellogg's. "Of course Father Thames has a continental breakfast, coffee and croissants."
>
> "My husband likes Grapenuts," I found myself saying feebly. Then, gathering strength, I asked, "And what do *you* have? An egg?"
>
> He shuddered. "Oh no—just black coffee and orange juice. I hate eggs."
>
> "Not Fabergé eggs, surely?" I said boldly, wondering if his face would change colour in some dramatic way.
>
> "Oh Mrs. Forsyth, how did you know about my little peccadillo?" he asked in an agitated tone. (*GB,* 16)

But Father Thames knows of Wilf's kleptomaniac pranks:

> "Oh yes, Bason borrows it every now and then. He doesn't realize that I know, of course. He thinks I don't notice." Father Thames smiled. "He is very fond of beautiful things, you know." (*GB,* 16)

There are no portraits of lesbians as such, but there are duos of women, sometimes one more "mannish" than the other,

from the first novel on—Edith Liversidge, who drops cigarette
ash into the tin of beans she is warming up for supper, and her
frail friend and relation, the harpist Connie Aspinall; or Mabel
Edgar and Charlotte Boniface in *Excellent Women;* or, in later
novels, the snorting Miss Clovis and her equally choleric friend
Gertrude Lydgate. They are far outnumbered in the gallery of
gayness by the men, whether closet or overt.

This emphasis on gay men rather than women may be statis-
tical or autobiographical or neither of these. In 1956 Barbara
Pym wrote in her diary (on the "Feast of St. Barbara"):

> On TV I thought that women have never been more terrifying
> than they are now—the curled head ("Italian style"), the paint
> and the jewellery, the exposed bosom—no wonder men turn
> to other men sometimes. (*VPE,* p. 197)

In *An Academic Question,* when the heroine, Caro, is asked by
Iris Horniblow if a mutual acquaintance, with the Firbankian
name of Coco, is heterosexual or other, Caro asks in turn, ". . .
are people to be classified as simply as that? Some people just
love themselves" (8). Sexual classification does tend to darken
counsel, and the vagaries of sexual conduct are not, in these
novels, a matter of moral judgment, only one of persistent comic
interest.

Barriers: Men on women; women on women; and women on men

> ". . . one's apt to forget that women consider themselves our
> equals now. But just occasionally one remembers that men
> were once the stronger sex," said Digby almost sadly. (*LA,* 6)

Digby and his friend Mark in *Less than Angels* are not beyond
redemption:

> "I shouldn't like my wife to do housework in the evenings,
> would you?"

"No, I suppose not, but women usually have their own way." (*LA,* 2)

These two are too young and humorous and speculative for their attitudes to have hardened or become engrained. One rather feels that they may, even if at present they incline to give women some credit here and there. Their fellow anthropologist, Tom, who is a bit older, can be more generous, though his comment is two-edged:

> He marvelled, as he had done before, at the sharpness of even the nicest of women. All except Deirdre; but she would learn, he supposed. (*LA,* 16)

Altogether the opposite sex is very opposite. "Women know what to do when you're ill," says Mervyn Cantrell in *An Unsuitable Attachment* (10), which shows what he thinks women are good for. Much older men think of "women" as "ladies." In *A Few Green Leaves* Dr. Gellibrand, the village physician, is giving a lecture on the "history of medical practice from the seventeenth century" and digresses wildly to comment upon twentieth-century athletic recreations:

> He was glad to notice that some younger men were taking up the practice of "jogging," as he believed it was called—it was a fine sight to see them trotting along on a winter morning. Ladies could do it too, no harm in that, but under medical supervision, of course. We couldn't have ladies dropping down dead, could we . . . ? (*FGL,* 31)

Mr. Mallett, a churchwarden in *Excellent Women,* is as blandly patriarchal as Dr. G.:

> "My good lady leaves the thinking to me," said Mr. Mallett, amid laughter from the men. (*EW,* 25)

Women are not supposed to think lest they risk the sort of put-down we hear from Fabian Driver, who says to Prudence, "I always think women who write books sound rather formidable" (*JP*, 10). Edwin Pettigrew believes that "anything to do with card indexes is more in a woman's line" (*UA*, 9). Wine, according to Aylwin Forbes, is men's territory; women shouldn't be "too knowledgeable" about it (*NFR*, 13).[2]

Nor are women rational in their emotions; they are like children, soft and silly. Men treat women as if they were childlike creatures from another planet. Prejudice is convenient against these aliens. The most generous attitude among men goes only so far as Everard Bone's remark in *Excellent Women,* melancholy and final as it sounds, "Women are quite impossible to understand sometimes" (16). Most men in the novels would have, or should have, omitted "sometimes." Or passed judgment in silence.

Nor do men talk much about other men; women, who men think talk too much, are far more interested in their own sex. In *Less than Angels* Catherine Oliphant—of whom Deirdre Swan says, "in the warm tone a woman unconsciously uses when praising another woman to a man," "I think she's awfully nice" (6)—Catherine is a romantic novelist, but in spite of this or because of it she is the shrewdest observer of her own sex:

> Men appeared to be so unsubtle, but perhaps it was only by contrast with the tortuous delicacy of women, who smothered their men under a cloud of sentimental associations—*our* song, *our* poem, *our* restaurant—till at last they struggled to break

2. But Rupert Stonebird doesn't sound like much of a connoisseur when he decides that "a sweet Spanish 'Sauterne'" is "quite a suitable choice" for a wedding reception; with judicious tolerance he remarks that "women are said to like sweet wines . . . though I think that's a fallacy" (*UA*, 23). Catherine Oliphant of *Less than Angels* likes to collect wine lists and clearly knows more about wine than the man in her life, Tom Mallow.

free, like birds trapped under the heavy black meshes of the strawberry net, she thought, changing her metaphor. (*LA*, 9)

And in a lighter mood:

"Yes, of course women do think the worst of each other, perhaps because only they can know what they are capable of. Men are regarded as being not quite responsible for their actions. Besides, they have other and more important things on their minds. Did you know that Tom was writing a thesis, for his Ph.D.?" (*LA*, 11)

However, for every one negative statement a woman makes about a woman there are a dozen positive ones. Mildred in *Excellent Women* says to Rocky, ". . . I suppose on the whole women don't make such a business of living as men do" (4). Jane in the next novel tells herself, ". . . that was why women were so wonderful; it was their love and imagination that transformed these unremarkable beings" (23). "These unremarkable beings" are of course men. And Catherine in the next novel tells her lover Tom, "Loneliness can often be a kind of strength in women, possibly in men too, of course, but it doesn't seem to show itself so much" (7). These comments are typical of her heroines, and of Barbara Pym herself. One finds entries in her notebooks like "With the years men get more bumbling and vague, but women get sharper" (MS PYM 45, p. 23) and "Women have a great (and perhaps tedious) capacity for devotion. Men ought really to be wary of awakening it" (MS PYM 46, p. 20).

Fascinating to a man, in fact to anyone, and remarkable for their detachment and observation are three passages concerning cosmetics. Here the subjection of women to men and women's strategies to attract them are painted for us as vividly as the women are painting themselves. In *Jane and Prudence*, Prudence and Jessie vie for that trivial man Fabian. Prudence is on her way to meeting him, and Jane is watching her preparations:

> She found herself quite unable to look at Prudence, whose
> eyelids were startlingly and embarrassingly green, glistening
> with some greasy preparation which had little flecks of silver in
> it. Was this what one had to do nowadays when one was un-
> married? she wondered. What hard work it must be, always
> remembering to add these little touches; there was something
> primitive about it, like the young African smearing himself
> with red cam-wood before he went courting. (*JP*, 9)

Jessie is on her way to seducing him:

> She worked carefully, smoothing on a peach-coloured founda-
> tion lotion, blending in rouge, powdering, outlining and fill-
> ing in her mouth, shading her eyelids with blue and darkening
> her lashes. (*JP*, 15)

And Mildred in *Excellent Women,* visiting a Ladies' Room in a
big department store, gives us a brilliant description that fore-
shadows the power and precision of *Quartet in Autumn:*

> Inside it was a sobering sight indeed and one to put us all in
> mind of the futility of material things and of our own mor-
> tality. *All flesh is but as grass . . .* I thought, watching the
> women working at their faces with savage concentration, open-
> ing their mouths wide, biting and licking their lips, stabbing at
> their noses and chins with powder-puffs. Some, who had
> abandoned the struggle to keep up, sat in chairs, their bodies
> slumped down, their hands resting on their parcels. One
> woman lay on a couch, her hat and shoes off, her eyes closed. I
> tiptoed past her with my penny in my hand. (*EW*, 14)

There is a quality beyond pathos here, beyond sexual attractions or antipathies, a thinner atmosphere than that of the busy
earthy sexual strife of the sexes.

Inevitably, since Barbara Pym was a woman and her protagonists are heroines not heroes, the range of comment made by women about men in the novels is voluminous, far more than that of men about women or women about women. What women think about men, one could even say, is what the novels are mostly about. Men do not turn out very well, generally speaking; in women's view they fail in a wide variety of ways.

One must be careful here to take into consideration just what woman is talking. We must be aware of her situation: if Helena Napier says, "Oh, yes, men are very simple and obvious in some ways, you know" (*EW*, 19), we remember that she is embroiled in battle with her husband, has been unsuccessful in acquiring an alternate lover, and thus is scarcely impartial. Or when Jessie Morrow in *Jane and Prudence* tells Fabian that "Women are very powerful—perhaps they are always triumphant in the end" (11), she is a powerful woman speaking to a weak man. Comment ranges in intelligence from Miss Doggett ("Men want only *one thing*") to the mature insights of Mildred or Jane or Catherine or Barbara Pym herself. In a letter to Robert Smith of December 8, 1963, she describes the reactions of another friend, Richard Roberts, to her writing:

> *E.W.* he found terribly sad, but witty—why is it that *men* find my books so sad? Women don't particularly. Perhaps they (men) have a slight guilt feeling that this is what they do to us, and yet really it isn't as bad as all that. (*VPE*, p. 223)

Later in life she wrote to Philip Larkin about a BBC interview:

> I did at least save myself once when a question about my treatment of men characters suggested that I had a low opinion of the sex. My instinctive reply sprang to my lips "Oh, but I *love* men," but luckily I realised how ridiculous it would sound, so said something feeble, but can't remember what." (July 9, 1977, *VPE*, p. 303)

Not only who says it and why, but also the scope of the animadversions varies. There are quibbles about the way men disarrange towels and splash water in a bathroom (*LA,* 3) and how they don't read poetry ("Men don't really go in for that sort of thing like women do" [*JP,* 17]) and how there are men who are always putting up shelves in the kitchen ("Sophia reflected, thinking how full of shelves some houses must be" [*UA,* 22]); and there are sweeping condemnations, like Dulcie's "Really, the ridiculousness of men!" (*NFR,* 15) or Jessie Morrow's (the woman of that name in *Crampton Hodnet,* not in *Jane and Prudence*) ". . . men *are* feeble, inefficient sorts of creatures (*CH,* 5) or Catherine's "I don't think we can ever hope to know all that goes on in a man's life or even to follow him with our loving thoughts, and perhaps that's just as well" (*LA,* 15).

Men, as Catherine implies, are morally inferior creatures. But it's not for ethical guidance that they need women. They want more than the one thing Miss Doggett is an authority on; they want food. In these novels women are the traditional "nurturers"; men much less strikingly and altogether unconsciously act out their own hallowed role of "providers."

Old-fashioned women like Miss Doggett are emphatic on the subject: "I think a man needs a cooked breakfast, especially after an all-night sitting in the House" (*JP,* 9), and that excellent woman, Mrs. Mayhew, is given to pronouncements like "Of course, a man must have meat" (*JP,* 3). Rhoda Wellcome finds it a "stable and comforting" idea that "the men must be fed" (*LA,* 21). Sister Dew's chief occupation seems to be supplying the nutritional needs of single men; she brings the bachelor Rupert Stonebird a steak and kidney pie and a plum cake (a man would like "something more substantial" than her celebrated sponge [*UA,* 22]). But not the wants of single women; she will not take her neighbor Ianthe a steak and kidney pie because ". . . one did not take cooked food to lone women in the same way as to lone men" (19). Belinda remarks that "men . . . just expect meals to appear on the table and they do (*STG*, 7).

Younger women are sceptical about the culinary helplessness of men, "a mistaken and old-fashioned concept," as Emma calls it (*FGL*, 18); yet this doesn't stop her from feeding them. Mildred is also sure that Everard Bone "would be quite equal to cooking a joint. Men are not nearly so helpless and pathetic as we sometimes like to imagine them" (*EW*, 23). Men get by with what they can. When Jane and Prudence have been busy in the kitchen with the dishwashing Nicholas and Fabian finally join them from the sitting room:

> "Yes, we should have offered sooner," said Fabian, "but I never feel I'm much good in a kitchen—not at the sink, anyway."
> "I never see why men should be good at cooking and yet not able to clear things up," said Prudence rather acidly. (*JP*, 17)

It's what anyone might not quite see. Yet the men go on being waited on, for everything from the meat they must have to proofreading and indexing. It is Prudence again, or is it Barbara Pym, who summarizes male prerogatives in food:

> Men alone, eating in a rather grand club with noble portals— and women alone, eating in a small, rather grimy restaurant which did a lunch for three and sixpence, including coffee. While Arthur Grampian [Prudence's boss] was shaking the red pepper on to his smoked salmon, Prudence was having to choose between the shepherd's pie and the stuffed marrow. (*JP*, 4)

The anatomy of men's failings occupies Prudence and every other heroine in the novels. Some weaknesses can be looked down on amiably enough; Catherine Oliphant "tended to regard most men, and Tom in particular, as children"; and her opinion of Alaric, the other man in her life, is that "Like so many men, he needed a woman stronger than himself" (*LA*, 2, 21).

And a woman can regard a man's isolation not without sympathy. Here is Miss Doggett again, this time a little more on target:

> "One does feel that men need company more than women do. A woman has a thousand and one little tasks in the house, and then her knitting or sewing." (*JP*, 11)

However, a woman cannot quite condone a man's laziness. Sister Blatt speaks out:

> "Father Malory help with the decorating! Those men never do anything. I expect they'll slink off and have a cup of coffee once the work starts." (*EW*, 13)

From Archdeacon Hoccleve to Graham Pettifer, men leave the work to women. Mildred's generalization about thankless tasks could have been made by all the heroines:

> "This may sound a cynical thing to say, but don't you think men sometimes leave difficulties to be solved by other people or to solve themselves?" (*EW*, 22)

There are moments of protest, as when Jane tells Fabian he himself must write to his cast-off, Prudence, that he is engaged to Jessie: "Men can't expect women to do quite everything for them" (*JP*, 19). But in general women do.

Men are selfish, egotistic, and vain. Milton is a figure who recurs in the novels, not as one of the "greater English poets" (in fact he is one of them who is never quoted), but because, as Jane mildly observes, "his treatment of women was not all that it should have been" (*JP*, 3). From Fabian, who puts his own photograph on his wife's grave, to Father Basil Branche, "one of those men who imagine that all women are running after them" (*UA*, 15), marriageable men preen themselves on their desirability.

In these novels courtship roles are often reversed; whether more or less than in life outside of novels is a moot point. Mildred recalls, in bare and effective language, a young man in her past:

> . . . and then the long country walks on Saturday afternoons and the talks about life and about himself. I did not remember that we had ever talked about me. (*EW*, 13)

Yet the worst male sin in these novels, and perhaps not only in them, is insensitivity. The urge to communicate is repulsed by insensitivity; it reduces a relationship to coarseness, a conversation to deafness and chatter, if there is no subtext of intuition and sympathy and openness. Stupidity is bad enough as a barrier, but forgivable; but "the economy of the closed heart" is not a genetic but a deliberate coldness. In her diary Barbara Pym once apostrophized a lover, "Oh, darling, how peculiarly insensitive your sex is!" (*VPE*, p. 125). Elsewhere: "How often do women have to listen to praise of other women and (if they are nice) just sit there agreeing. And yet men don't do it maliciously, just in their simplicity" (*VPE*, p. 225). "Natural male conceit" (*NFR*, 22) enchains a man, and it is the most jarring note in women's attempted harmonies.

From all these hearty antagonisms one might conclude that a man or woman would burst out like Moloch, in Barbara Pym's unquoted Milton, "My sentence is for open war!" But they need each other, and in Barbara Pym's novels this is the imperative, a dark one, of their bright encounters.

God and Miss Pym

The Church

All Saints' today, then All Souls'; everybody could share in the commemoration of the saints and the departed. Then would come Advent followed closely—too closely, it often seemed—by Christmas. After Christmas came Boxing Day, the Feast of St. Stephen, hardly observed as such unless it happened to be one's patronal festival; then the Innocents, St. John the Evangelist and Epiphany. The Conversion of St. Paul and Candlemass (where one usually sang one of Keble's less felicitous hymns) were followed all too soon by the Sundays before Lent, but the evenings were drawing out. Ash Wednesday was an important landmark—evening Mass and the Imposition of Ashes, the black smudge on the forehead, "dust thou art and to dust shalt thou return"—some people didn't like that, thought it "morbid" or "not very nice." . . .

Everybody knew about Lent, of course, even if they didn't do anything about it, with Palm Sunday ushering in the services of Holy Week—not what they used to be, certainly, but there was still something left of Maundy Thursday, Good Friday and Holy Saturday with the ceremonies, the prelude to Easter Day. Low Sunday always seemed a bit of an anticlimax after all that had gone before but it wasn't long before Ascension Day and then Whit Sunday or Pentecost as it was properly called. After that you had Corpus Christi, with a procession out of doors if fine, and then Trinity Sunday, fol-

lowed by all those long hot summer Sundays, with the green
vestments and the occasional saint's day. . . . That was how it
had always been and how it would go on in spite of trendy
clergy trying to introduce so-called up-to-date forms of worship, rock and roll and guitars and discussions about the Third
World instead of evensong. (*QA*, 8)

Edwin lingers over the church year just as Ianthe Broome
does: "It gave her a comfortable glow to think of the church
and the life that went on around it, dear and familiar and with
the same basic pattern everywhere" (*UA*, 2).

The novels are full of the ecclesiastical, from Paschal candles
to Asperges, from Crockford's to the *Church Times*, but they
are nearly empty of openly recounted spiritual experience. Reviewers noticed this from the beginning, particularly, as one
might expect, those in the *Church Times:*

> But the religious aspect of the story never succeeds in penetrat-
> ing beneath the surface of a slightly precious and unworthy
> ecclesiasticism. As a novel deliberately set in a minor key, *A
> Glass of Blessings* has its points. But the tinkling of teacups is no
> substitute for the ringing of tocsins. (June 13, 1958)

Several critics commented on the silent tocsins when Barbara
Pym's diaries, notebooks, and letters were published in *A Very
Private Eye* in 1984. Rosemary Dinnage in the *New York Review
of Books:*

> We do not know anything about Barbara Pym's faith . . .
> Clearly it was central to her life. (August 16, 1984, p. 16)

James Fenton in *The Times:*

> Attendance at church service seems to have supplied most
> other deficiencies in her life. I say attendance rather than reli-
> gion, since it is only very rarely that you get any sense of a
> spiritual inner life. (July 19, 1984)

And Victoria Glendinning in the *New York Times Book Review:*

> Perhaps her faith sustained her as she advanced into middle
> age; but though we read a lot about the churches she at-
> tended, their furnishings, practices, and incumbents, we learn
> nothing about her God. (July 8, 1984, p. 3)

Yet one can piece her faith together from rare moments in the
novels, and from more frequent comments, as one would expect, in the diaries. The sole example in the novels that I have
found of inner as opposed to outer religion is the conversion of
Rupert Stonebird in *An Unsuitable Attachment.* He is a clergyman's son who had lost his faith at Oxford:

> And now, eighteen years afterwards, in a poorly attended
> North London church of hideous architecture and amid clouds
> of strong incense, he seemed to have regained that faith. It had
> been an uncomfortable and disturbing sensation . . . (*UA,* 3)

These few words are as close as we come to an account of a
religious crisis. One thinks what Mrs. Humphry Ward would
have made of it (or rather one prefers not to).

Surely it was not that Barbara Pym wanted to avoid the "uncomfortable and disturbing" that might have marred the detachment of her tone. Simply it is an area in which she did not
jest—it was not her literary caution but her faith, which she
believed should be private, not paraded in print. She obeyed
the Third Commandment.

Speaking as herself in her diaries she could be more forth-
right, and even sprightly:

> Odd it is how few words rhyme with "God" in our language
> and rather unsuitable ones like sod and trod . . . (MS PYM
> 46, p. 5)

What different conceptions one could have of God according

to the country one was in—those sun-baked cemeteries in
Marseilles. (July 2, 1955, *VPE*, p. 195)

But are Christians always and necessarily pleasant people?
Who could like the wise virgins in the Bible, for example? Is
that one of the trials of it all—that one must be prepared to be
disliked? (MS PYM 44, p. 19)

She did not want a reader to dislike her novels. And that other
writers both poets and novelists have displayed their faith or
lack of it is beside the point; it was not in her to do so.

". . . rock and roll and guitars and discussions about the
Third World instead of evensong": not in her own person but
in believers like Edwin is the decline of the Church observed.
That their own regrets are hers is clear in itself and corrobo-
rated by the diaries. I don't doubt that she especially shared
Edwin's sort of dry melancholy:

He often thought regretfully of those days of the Anglo-
Catholic revival in the last century and even the more sympa-
thetic climate of twenty years ago, where Father G., tall and
cadaverous in cloak and biretta, would have been rather more
in place than in the church of the nineteen seventies where so
many of the younger priests went in for jeans and long hair.
(*QA*, 1)

Edwin notes the dwindling congregations as he makes his
rounds of London churches:

The attendance at the sung Mass had been pretty much as
usual for a weekday—only seven in the congregation but the
full complement in the sanctuary. (*QA*, 1)

And in the country too, as Piers and Wilmet are aware in *A
Glass of Blessings*:

"I may as well come to the service with you," he said, "though country churches always depress me."

"Yes, I know what you mean. There is something sad about them, as if their life were all in the past—those tablets and monuments of the eighteenth and nineteenth centuries, leaving no room for modern ones." (*GB*, 3)

It is one of Wilmet's nostalgias, and, for some of us, one of ours.

Clergyman and churchgoer   The gamut of clergymen runs from High to Low, with many of the former hovering on the line between Anglo-Catholicism and Roman Catholicism but never teetering over into it. There are many more High than Low, which is accounted for by Barbara Pym's own persuasion.

She is very amusing indeed on the superstitions about Roman Catholicism that cloud the minds of some of her characters. An upper-class woman, Bertha Burdon in *An Unsuitable Attachment,* deplores the life her sister and her niece Ianthe had led in the Victoria part of London:

"But there they were living on top of each other in that flat, *much* too near Westminster Cathedral—I always felt it most oppressive when I went to see them, the cathedral towering over them like that. And one could even see the canons going in and out—*Roman* canons, of course . . ." (*UA,* 20)

A middle-class woman in *Excellent Women,* Dora Caldicote, is disgusted by almost everything about the Roman Catholic abbey which she and Mildred visit:

"I hope you didn't put any money in any of those boxes," she said. "They've got a shop round the corner to sell rosaries and images and all sorts of highly-coloured junk. I can't imagine why anybody should want to buy such stuff." (*EW,* 21)

And down the social scale to Mrs. Morris, Mildred's Welsh cleaning woman:

"Well, it was my sister Gladys and her husband, been staying
with us they have. I took them to church Sunday evening and
they didn't like it at all, nor the incense, said it was Roman
Catholic or something and we'd all be kissing the Pope's toes
before you could say knife." (*EW*, 3)

They vary in crudity, but the gist is the same. Barbara Pym herself liked a church that was as high as it could be without being
Roman Catholic. She is witty about this preference in her letters to Robert Smith:

> One doesn't quite know where one is with church things. St.
> Laurence's is not exactly in the forefront where ceremonies are
> concerned and we have Series I where everyone else has Series
> II. Some people don't even cross themselves at the end of the
> Creed now (I mean people who always did). And of course no
> kneeling at the Incarnation. I said I would go on, didn't I, but
> now feel that for a rheumaticky woman of nearly 56 a low bow
> is more comfortable. (April 6, 1969, MS PYM 162/1)

> Yesterday we went to St. Augustine's, Kilburn—I suppose you
> must have been there? It is a fine building and of course lovely
> to have a proper sung High Mass with *three* priests. The con-
> gregation seemed rather elderly but this was the 11 o'clock—I
> imagine the 9.45, also a sung Mass, would be more swinging.
> (May 25, 1970, MS PYM 162/1)

If there is an average clergyman in Barbara Pym's novels, he is
a kindly man, given more to reflection than doctrine, more to
jumble sales than dogma or proselytizing or making calls on his
parishioners, who are usually busy watching the box. He may
be cherished, but rather than a shepherd he is rather sheeplike
himself. He is sincere, benevolent, and ineffectual.

Usually the clergy are tolerant of one another. But not always. Father Plowman, who is very High, is uncomfortable

with Archdeacon Hoccleve, who is very literary:

> It was such a pity, Belinda reflected, that clergymen were so apt to bring out the worst in each other, especially with the season of Peace and Goodwill so near. As a species they did not *get on* . . . (*STG*, 18)

Yet the Archdeacon does not get on well with anyone except Belinda, and even with her he has irascible moments. Her sister Harriet is not one of Hoccleve's fans:

> "If it weren't so far to walk," she said, "I should certainly go to Edward Plowman's church; he does at least preach good homely sermons that everyone can understand. He works systematically through the Ten Commandments and the Beatitudes, I believe; much the most sensible thing to do. Besides he's such a nice man." (*STG*, 2)

Even nicer is Harriet's favorite, the new curate Mr. Donne, whom she defends to the Archdeacon on the occasion of the vicarage garden party, which is complete with stalls:

> "He is an excellent preacher," said Harriet stoutly, if irrelevantly, "and he seems to have the coconuts *very* well organized. Now Mr. Donne," she called, bringing him into the group, "don't forget that you promised to let me win a coconut."
> "Ah, Miss Bede, I'm sure your skill will win the biggest one of all," said Mr. Donne gallantly. (*STG*, 2)

Unfortunately for our entertainment, not many of the clergymen are quite so eccentric as the Archdeacon or so absurd as his curate. Perhaps in a later novel, *Jane and Prudence,* Nicholas Cleveland is being ironic when he says,

> "A clergyman in the Church of England should be ready for every emergency, from Asperges and Incense to North End Position and Evening Communion." (*JP*, 22)

But probably not; they are marooned among the minutiae of
their office. They may be exemplary, devout, and devoted, but
what we hear is how human they are, by which I mean petty:

> "A friend of mine knew a clergyman who used to have *bouil-
> labaisse* flown over specially from Marseilles every Ash Wednes-
> day. I don't call *that* self denial." (*UA*, 8)

In other words they are no different from their parishioners.
Barbara Pym summed up the pastor and his flock in a letter to
Robert Smith:

> You thought perhaps that I might have retained some idealised
> vision of the clergy and perhaps in a sense I still do, just as I
> still even now at my age tend to believe what people tell me—
> it's just a quality in oneself. But I am under no illusion about
> church people, on the whole, and the dullness and pettiness
> and dreariness of all the things a clergyman would have to do.
> (*VPE*, p. 245)

Nor was she under any more illusion about people who go
to church than about those who don't. When Letty of *Quartet
in Autumn* is "arranging the rest of her life" and contemplating
"getting involved" in the church, her thoughts center around
central heating:

> Easter was of course better, with daffodils in the church and
> people making an effort with their clothes, but Whitsun was
> bitterly cold, with a leaden grey sky and the church heating
> turned off. Did people then only go for the light and warmth,
> the coffee after the Sunday morning service and a friendly
> word from the vicar? (*QA*, 16)

Why indeed do they go? Even among the excellent women
faith does not conquer all, and Mildred Lathbury, who is
among the best of them, is saddened at how belief is buried
under bickering:

I suddenly felt very tired and thought how all over England, and perhaps, indeed, anywhere where there was a church and a group of workers, these little frictions were going on. Somebody else decorating the pulpit when another had always done it, somebody's gift of flowers being relegated to an obscure window, somebody's cleaning of the brasses being criticised when she had been doing them for over thirty years. . . . And now Lady Farmer's lilies on the floor and peonies on the altar, an unheard-of thing! (*EW*, 22)

It makes the nonbelievers' cynicism refreshing:

"And anyway, why should the Church want to get anywhere?" said Rocky. "I think it's much more comforting to think of it staying just where it is."
"Wherever that may be," Helena added. (*EW*, 6)

On the one hand, there are the cynics like the Napiers; on the other, the attractive "agnostics" like Sybil in *A Glass of Blessings;* and there are, really worse than the others, the bland and superficial, who indulge themselves by escape into platitude:

"Of course a lot of very *good* people aren't religious in the sense of being church-goers," persisted Mrs. Bonner.
"No, I know they aren't," I agreed, feeling that at any moment she would begin talking about it being just as easy to worship God in a beechwood or on the golf links on a fine Sunday morning.
"I must admit I always feel the presence of God much more when I'm in a garden or on a mountain," she continued.
"I'm afraid I haven't got a garden and am really never on a mountain," I said. (*EW*, 6)

Mr. Latimer, the curate in *Crampton Hodnet,* sums up the dismal picture of the churchgoer:

Yes, this was the Church of England, his flock, thought Mr. Latimer, a collection of old women, widows and spinsters,

and one young man not quite right in the head. These were
the people among whom he was destined to spend his life.
(*CH*, 10)

What is left, by a process of negative definition, is the recon-
ciled and real believer, like Barbara Pym.

Barbara Pym   It is a solitary position, that of the believer,
but it sustains, and it makes a still center for the swirling vicissi-
tudes of life around one. In *Less than Angels* Rhoda Wellcome
and her sister Mabel Swan are listening to a radio play:

> After a while both the sisters realized that they had heard it
> before, but neither could remember exactly how it ended. So
> life seemed to go round in a circle, with tables hurtling
> through the air. (*LA*, 3)

The people in these novels spend their time trying to "connect," to "make contact" with one another, to "communicate,"
but such efforts in the final perspective are quite futile, and this
is not the least of the ironies we have encountered. In *An Unsuitable Attachment* Rupert has escorted his neighbor Ianthe to
her home and returns to his own:

> Oh, this coming back to an empty house, Rupert thought,
> when he had seen her safely up to her door. People—though
> perhaps it was only women—seemed to make so much of it.
> As if life itself were not as empty as the house one was coming
> back to. (*UA*, 3)

Man is a social animal, and woman is much more so; but the
most energetic and curious of them end up baffled and their
efforts at understanding others are as grass. Catherine Oliphant
(life is "comic and sad and indefinite") confesses:

> Understanding somebody else's filing system is just about as
> easy as really getting to know another human being. Just when
> you think you know everything about them, there's the impos-

sible happening, the M for Miscellaneous when you naturally assumed it would be under something else. (*LA,* 9)

Later Catherine will attempt to reintroduce Alaric Lydgate to human relationships, but till then he is the extreme, even cynical, example of the antisocial. He likes to retreat inside an African mask:

> He often sat like this in the evenings, withdrawing himself from the world, feeling in the stuffy darkness of the mask that he was back again in his native-built house, listening to the rain falling outside. He often thought what a good thing it would be if the wearing of masks or animals' heads could become customary for persons over a certain age. How restful social intercourse would be if the face did not have to assume any expression—the strained look of interest, the simulated delight or surprise, the anxious concern one didn't really feel. (*LA,* 5)

It is impossible to turn away from other people, but to turn inward into one's self can heal and nurture and sustain. It is what Barbara Pym did, I think, and I think it accounts for the way her novels end, not exactly roseate, but tinged with hope. Even the bleakest of them, *Quartet in Autumn,* is still a comedy, and its heroine, Letty, realizes at the very end of her story that "life still held infinite possibilities for change." When Barbara Pym was once asked if she shared Letty's tentative optimism, she said, "Certainly. One isn't forgotten. One may seem to be. But not by God" (interview, *Eastern Times,* May 25, 1978).

She is an unfashionably, even uniquely affirmative writer. She is brave enough to say yes. This may be the ultimate satisfaction of her comedies, that, despite what she knows about our vanity, idleness, and egotism, they are documents of faith and acceptance.

Index